BY OATH CONSIGNED

By the same author:
Treaty of the Great King

BY OATH CONSIGNED

*A Reinterpretation of the Covenant Signs
of Circumcision and Baptism*

by

MEREDITH G. KLINE
*Professor of Old Testament
Gordon Divinity School*

WILLIAM B. EERDMANS PUBLISHING COMPANY
GRAND RAPIDS, MICHIGAN

Copyright © 1968 by Wm. B. Eerdmans Publishing Co.
All rights reserved
Library of Congress Catalog Card Number: 67-19329
Printed in the United States of America

To Paul Woolley

PREFACE

A recognition of the clear correspondence, both formal and functional, between the Old Testament covenant rite of circumcision and the ratification ceremonies of ancient Near Eastern treaties, and subsequently a persuasion that here, too, was the cultural context in which the New Testament rite of baptism must be reinterpreted, led to the preparation of an article on this theme several years ago. It soon became evident, however, that such a study would better follow upon a broader, introductory analysis of the nature of the divine covenants of Scripture. The result was two articles published in *The Westminster Theological Journal*, the first called "Law Covenant" (XXVII, 1 [Nov., 1964], 1-20) and the second "Oath and Ordeal Signs" (XXVII, 2 [May, 1965], 115-139 and XXVIII, 1 [Nov., 1965], 1-37). The present publication is a revised version of those articles, and for the privilege of the use here made of them I would express my appreciation to the editors of that journal.

Since 1964-5, research on the international treaties of the ancient Near East and their relationship to certain biblical covenants has continued to flourish, as indeed it has for over a decade now, but without the appearance elsewhere (to my knowledge) of an independent and extended inquiry into the possible significance of this research for our theological understanding of the biblical sacrament-signs of circumcision and baptism. In fact, the orientation of the investigators' interest has in general been largely historical and literary. The relatively neglected theological implications of the new information invite further attention, and who should pursue the possibilities with more curiosity and anticipation than those who are sympathetically concerned about the development of Covenant Theology?

This book is dedicated to Paul Woolley, academician *par excellence*, with heartiest thanks for his expert editorial oversight of the present work in its original form and of my other writings that have appeared in *The Westminster Theological Journal*. They have all benefited from the precision, encyclopedic knowledge, and wisdom that he brings to this task. What I have most appreciated, however, is that Professor Woolley can always be counted on to be a kindred spirit in any adventure in quest of a fresh presentation of the biblical faith.

The following paragraph introduced the "Oath and Ordeal Signs" article, and I still cherish—fondly, if faintly—the hope expressed towards its close:

A more authentic identification of the covenant signs of circumcision and baptism has been made possible through the recovery of their original historical context of covenant form and ceremony. It will be found that the new view of these rites opened up to us by our improved historical perspective challenges the divergent ecclesiastical traditions, not merely at distinctive points peculiar to one or another communion but, more significantly, in respect to that which has been their area of (at least formal) agreement. Specifically, the traditional consensus that these sacramental symbols are primarily if not exclusively signs of divine grace and blessing is now called in question. And perhaps in this there is cause for hope. For if it should really be the case that our common foundations are being shaken under us by advances in historical knowledge, it could prove difficult to maintain our composedly adamant stance of antagonism over against each other. We might find ourselves tumbling together, head over traditions.

Good friends have duly warned me that the title I have given this book sounds as though it was in part stolen from C. S. Lewis and in part lifted out of some commercial docket, and further that it will not communicate to the man browsing in the book stall. They are in all probability right on all scores. But something a little different in the way of a title is not easy to come by any more. Besides, this word "consign" has at least an interesting past; for it has been used for fateful transactions involving sacred signs and holy oaths—the world of ideas in which this book moves. Maybe the word is due then for theological rehabilitation; in any case, the idea is.

For his considerateness shown throughout the entire publishing process I would express gratitude to Mr. William B. Eerdmans,

Jr. My thanks go also to Miss Linda Dyer for the preparation of the typescript.

Biblical quotations are from the Authorized Version except as otherwise specified. Translations of passages from other ancient texts not documented in the footnotes are the author's own.

—MEREDITH G. KLINE

Hamilton, Massachusetts
January, 1967

CONTENTS

Preface	7
One: OATH AND COVENANT	13
I. Old Testament Usage	14
II. New Testament Usage	22
Two: LAW COVENANT	26
I. Pre-Redemptive Covenant	26
II. The Priority of Law	29
III. Covenant and Kingdom	36
Three: CIRCUMCISION: OATH-SIGN OF THE OLD COVENANT	39
I. Malediction	39
II. Consecration	43
Four: JOHN'S BAPTISMAL SIGN OF JUDGMENT	50
I. Messenger of Ultimatum	51
II. Symbolic Water Ordeal	55
Five: CHRISTIAN BAPTISM: OATH-SIGN OF THE NEW COVENANT	63
I. Baptism as Ordeal	65
II. New Covenant Judgment	73
Six: THE ADMINISTRATION OF CIRCUMCISION AND BAPTISM	84
I. Vassal Authority in Covenant Administration	84
II. Circumcision and Generation	86
III. The Authority Principle and Baptism	90
Indexes	103

CHAPTER ONE

OATH AND COVENANT

Following the lead of the Scriptures themselves, Reformed theology has long prized the covenant as a structural concept for integrating all that God has so diversely spoken unto men of old time and in these last days.

A recent writer, comparing the relationship of law and gospel within the Lutheran and Reformed traditions, finds the genius of the Reformed position in this overarching status it accords to the covenant.[1] He acknowledges that in Lutheran thinking, especially when there is an insistence on the exclusively negative purpose of law to mortify and condemn, law and gospel remain in tension. And he grants that a relative harmony of law and gospel is achieved under the vault of the covenant concept in Reformed thought; in this setting law, like gospel, has a vivifying use, for law is here the obligation to covenant service that attends election to covenant privilege.

While recognizing indeed that privilege brings responsibility, Reformed theologians would want to trace the roots of law's demands in holy depths beyond covenantal election. They would also want to affirm that the compatibility of law and gospel-promise is discernible in more than the instructional, so-called third

---

[1] Gustav Wingren, "Law and Gospel and Their Implications for Christian Life and Worship," *Studia Theologica*, 17, 2 (1963), 77-89. Wingren observes that in the Westminster Confession of Faith the Covenant of Grace from one point of view stands above law and gospel. For an example of Lutheran utilization of the covenant for the systematizing of biblical teaching see W. R. Roehrs, "Covenant and Justification in the Old Testament," *Concordia Theological Monthly*, 35 (1964), 583-602.

use of the law. Nevertheless, the observation is of course correct that in Reformed theology the covenant concept has figured conspicuously in the correlation of law and gospel. In fact, before the end of the sixteenth century a growing biblical insight within the movement of Covenant Theology had embraced all special revelation, pre-redemptive as well as redemptive, in the unity of a covenant framework.

It is the purpose of the present chapter to show that historical usage justifies the meaning that necessarily attaches to the term "covenant" when applied in the comprehensive fashion just mentioned, and it will be the purpose of the second chapter to make proposals towards a more systematically coherent formulation of the theology of the covenant. Such a study might serve as an introduction to a general survey of the successive divine covenants of biblical history. Here, however, it will perform the more limited function of providing the necessary foundation for an investigation of the covenant signs of circumcision and baptism.

I. OLD TESTAMENT USAGE

If we would preserve a substantial continuity between our theological use of terms and the biblical usage, we must inquire what kind of divine-human relationship was called "covenant" in the biblical world. To determine this is largely a matter of surveying the data of the Bible itself. For within the biblical world the conceptualizing of the relationship between a religious community and its deity as one founded on a covenantal engagement was confined (with perhaps certain inferentially supported exceptions) to the case of the God of the Bible and his people. But our historical survey will also take account of some extra-biblical covenants that exhibit parallels to the form of several biblical covenants and hence clarify our understanding of them.

Walther Eichrodt in his standard work on Old Testament theology (in which, as is well known, he assigns the central and unifying position in the religious thinking of the Old Testament to the concept of the covenant) calls attention to the multiformity of arrangement that was known as "covenant." Appealing especially to the Sinaitic transactions as evidence of bilateral relationship in the covenant-union between Yahweh and Israel, Eichrodt concludes: "The idea that in ancient Israel the $b^e r\bar{\imath}t$ was always and only thought of as Yahweh's pledging of himself, to which human effort was required to make no kind of response (Kraetzschmar), can therefore be proved to be erroneous."[2] Then, after tracing the history of the covenant concept, he summarizes: "One cannot help being aware that the term has to cover two lines of thought along which the meaning has developed. The first runs from 'covenant' through 'covenant relationship', 'covenant precept' and 'legal system' to 'religion', 'cultus' and 'covenant people'; the other from 'covenant' through the divine act of 'establishment', 'the relationship of grace' and 'revelation' to the 'order of redemption', the 'decree of salvation' and the final 'consummation of all things'."[3]

Eichrodt's reconstruction of the development of Israel's theological thought is of course controlled by his modern approach to biblical revelation and the higher criticism of Scripture, but his twofold analysis does reflect an actual duality in the pertinent covenantal data of the Bible. The one-sided approach criticized by Eichrodt has continued to find advocacy.[4] Among orthodox theologians, too, there has been a line of those who would frame the covenant concept in unilateral fashion with exclusive emphasis on the divine initiative and promise, without, however, denying the responsibility of the covenant recipients.[5] Although we shall keep an eye on the various questions being raised in the numerous current covenant studies, our interaction here will be primarily with this development within the orthodox tradition in the hope of providing a corrective for its one-sided formulations of this fundamental biblical theme.

It is not necessary to examine more than a few of the biblical examples of divine covenants in order to demonstrate that there is precedential justification in biblical terminology for designating law administration and dispensation of promise alike as "covenant" and to vindicate thereby the comprehensive application

---

[2] *Theology of the Old Testament* (Philadelphia, 1961), I, 37 (translation of Volume I of *Theologie des Alten Testaments,* 6th ed. [Stuttgart, 1959]). The critical reference in the above quotation from Eichrodt is to R. Kraetzschmar, *Die Bundesvorstellung im AT* (Marburg, 1896).

[3] *Ibid.*, p. 66.

[4] See, *e.g.*, J. Begrich, "*berit.* Ein Beitrag zur Erfassung einer alttestamentlichen Denkform," *Zeitschrift für die alttestamentliche Wissenschaft,* 60 (1944), 1-11.

[5] See, *e.g.*, John Murray, *The Covenant of Grace* (London, 1954). Murray would define any and all covenants made by God with men by the restrictive formula: "a sovereign administration of grace and promise" (p. 31).

of the term as representing a proper and natural systematization of biblical revelation. First, however, notice must be taken of a feature which law covenants and promise covenants have in common but which, nevertheless, being more closely analyzed, serves to distinguish clearly between the two. Every divine-human covenant in Scripture involves a sanction-sealed commitment to maintain a particular relationship or follow a stipulated course of action. In general, then, a covenant may be defined as a relationship under sanctions. The covenantal commitment is characteristically expressed by an oath sworn in the solemnities of covenant ratification.[6] Both in the Bible and in extra-biblical documents concerned with covenant arrangements the swearing of the oath is frequently found in parallelistic explication of the idea of entering into the covenant relationship, or as a synonym for it.

It is this swearing of the ratificatory oath that provides an identification mark by which we can readily distinguish in the divine covenants of Scripture between a law covenant and one of promise. For it is evident that if God swears the oath of the ratification ceremony, that particular covenantal transaction is one of promise, whereas if man is summoned to swear the oath, the particular covenant thus ratified is one of law. In view of questions that have emerged in the course of the development of Covenant Theology, it is especially to be observed that precisely because it is sworn commitment that constitutes these particular transactions "covenants," a relationship ratified by a human oath of allegiance is a "covenant" because of that human oath, and it is a "covenant," therefore, quite irrespective of whether or not the arrangement happens to be at the same time an administration of divine grace and promise.

Genesis 15 provides an example of a covenant sealed by divine oath. The theophany-ritual described there symbolized the conditional self-malediction that inheres in the swearing of oaths. To his promise to Abraham God added a second immutable thing (Heb. 6:17, 18). Passing between the slain and divided beasts

[6] Geerhardus Vos affirms in his *Biblical Theology* (Grand Rapids, 1948) that the reason for calling the relation established between God and Israel at Sinai a "covenant" is found "entirely in the ceremony of ratification" (p. 137). He concludes concerning the covenant concept that the "only common idea, always present, is that of a solemn religious sanction" (p. 277; *cf.* p. 33). In his valuable study, *Treaty and Covenant* (Rome, 1963), Dennis J. McCarthy states that the covenant was "the means the ancient world took to extend relationships beyond the natural unity by blood" (p. 175) and that the basic idea of it was "a union based on an oath" (p. 96).

beneath the threatening birds of prey (cf. vv. 9-11, 17), God invoked the curse of the oath upon himself should he prove false to it. That curse, so effectively portrayed by the combined ritual and natural features of the scene, was a common one among ancient treaty-curses. In an eighth-century treaty of Bar-ga'ayah with Mati'el the symbolic meaning of a rite like that of Genesis 15 is verbally set forth: "[And just as] (40) this calf is cut to pieces, so may Mati'el be cut to pieces and his nobles be cut to pieces" (Sefireh, I, A). And the sequel already threatening in Genesis 15 finds expression as a curse in the seventh-century vassal treaty of Esarhaddon: "[May Ninurta, chief of the gods] . . . feed your flesh to the eagle (and) jackal" (lines 425-427).[7] By undergoing this ritual God declared in effect that if he failed to fulfill the promises of the covenant (cf. vv. 5, 14, 16, 18ff.), he was like these creatures to be slain and devoured as a feast for the fowls. Thus, on that day the Lord ratified a covenant with Abraham (v. 18), a covenant that was a dispensation of grace and blessing guaranteed by twofold immutability.[8]

Exodus 24 contains the record of the ratification ceremony of another divine covenant. On this occasion, however, the oath was sworn by the people of Israel, not by the Lord. It was an oath of allegiance by which they devoted themselves to the service of their sovereign Lord according to all the law he had revealed to them (v. 7). Some have contested calling this affirmation made by Israel an oath, but if due weight is given to all the factors present in the situation there need be no hesitation on that score.[9] In any case, it is clear that the solemn commitment by which this covenant was ratified was not made by the Lord but by Israel.

---

[7] Cf. Jer. 34:19f.; Deut. 28:26; I Sam. 17:44ff. See further D. R. Hillers, *Treaty-Curses and the Old Testament Prophets* (Rome, 1964), under the heading, "No Burial" (pp. 68f.).

[8] Note the boundary survey in Gen. 15:18ff. In several of the extra-biblical treaties there are geographical sections listing the cities and describing the borders which the suzerain confirmed to the vassal. Cf. my *Treaty of the Great King* (Grand Rapids, 1963), p. 23 (hereafter abbreviated *TGK*); K. Baltzer, *Das Bundesformular* (Neukirchen, 1960), pp. 21f., 30; and McCarthy, *op. cit.*, pp. 58f., 64. This feature of the land survey and grant constitutes an important element in other biblical covenants; for example, Deuteronomy and Joshua 24. In the latter case this covenantal feature has had a broad historiographical impact on the whole book in which it is recorded (cf. especially chaps. 12ff.). The roots of the biblical motif, it may be added, are found in Gen. 1:28.

[9] Cf. *TGK*, pp. 15f.

The systematic theologian must beware lest his proper concern for the unity and continuity of the divine covenants or for the sovereignty of God in the covenant relationship blur or even virtually obliterate in his thought the distinct identity of the Sinaitic Covenant as a particular administration with its own historical beginning in a concrete occasion of covenant making.[10] It is true that even prior to the covenant making at Sinai the Israelites were in a covenant relationship to God by virtue of the terms of God's covenant with Abraham and his seed. It is also true that a passage like Exodus 19:5, 6 with its explicit mention of the covenant indicates that it was the continuing or even consummating realization of the blessing sanctions of the covenant, not the original making of the covenant, that had to wait for Israel's keeping of the stipulations. It is true, too, that the covenant administration of Exodus 19–24 must be understood as serving a purpose compatible with the on-going program of redemptive grace. The very blood rite by which this covenant was ratified (Ex. 24:5ff.) implicitly involved, according to the interpretation of it elsewhere in the Scriptures (see Hebrews 9:18ff.), a divine promise of forgiving and purifying grace. Nevertheless, it is not true that the Sinaitic Covenant was conceived of as already formally dispensed and operative prior to the episode described in Exodus 19–24. Rather, these chapters are precisely the record of the process of dispensing or making that particular covenant by oath and sacrifice (*cf.* Ps. 50:5). And the decisive feature in the covenanting process at Sinai, the act of sworn commitment, was performed by Israel. Even the sacrificial ritual, which typologically conveyed the divine promise, must be understood in this historico-legal context as paradoxically serving the further function of dramatizing symbolically the curse sanction invoked in Israel's ratificatory oath against the defaulter. We are bound to conclude, then, that the covenantal transaction of Exodus 19–24 cannot be defined in terms of a unilateral promissory commitment from the divine side. This particular engagement was, on the contrary, constituted a covenant by Israel's formal pledging of obedience to God's law. It was a law covenant.

The book of Deuteronomy is the documentary witness to an-

[10] The observations at this point above take account especially of the discussion of the matter by John Murray; see *op. cit.*, pp. 20ff. Though venturing to differ from Prof. Murray in this regard, I would like to acknowledge with appreciation indebtedness to him for illumination of the things of most import in our relationship to our covenant Lord.

other such law, or vassal, covenant. In it Moses issued the solemn summons to Israel to swear the ratificatory oath: "Ye stand this day all of you before the Lord your God . . . that thou shouldest enter into covenant with the Lord thy God, and into his oath" (Deut. 29:10a, 12a; *cf.* 29:14; 26:17-19; 27:15-26). It has been argued on the basis of one translation of Deuteronomy 26:17ff. that the Deuteronomic Covenant was a contract based on a bilateral oath.[11] Verses 17a and 18a are construed as saying that Israel has caused Yahweh to pledge and Yahweh has caused Israel to pledge. If, however, the Massoretic text is allowed to stand, that interpretation is made difficult by the remaining content of these verses. For an oath taken by God would hardly consist in demands imposed on Israel (latter part of v. 17), and an oath taken by Israel would not likely stress the divine promise (vv. 18b, 19). Preferable, therefore, is an interpretation such as that reflected in the major English versions; thus, "You have declared this day concerning the Lord that he is your God . . . and the Lord has declared this day concerning you that you are a people for his own possession" (vv. 17a, 18a, *RSV*). These verses are to be understood, then, not as a description of the ratificatory oath ritual as such but as a summation of the general significance of this covenantal engagement.

Such a summation, it should be added, does remind us that the Deuteronomic Covenant, considered within its broader historical framework and even in terms of its own total contents, contains the element of divine promise. In fact, embedded among Deuteronomy's prophetic prospects is a divine oath guaranteeing the promise (Deut. 32:40ff.). Thus, there is grace along with law, the Deuteronomic renewal of the Sinaitic Covenant being similar to the latter in this respect, as we should naturally expect. Nevertheless, when we have in view the particular verbal and ritual process of ratification that transpired on a certain day in the plains of Moab and by which the Deuteronomic Covenant was constituted a covenant, then we must say that this covenant was based on Israel's oath of allegiance rather than on a bilateral oath. Certainly there is nothing at this point similar to the theophanic action of Genesis 15. Nor is the place occupied by the divine oath in Deuteronomy 32:40 the same as that of the central and constitutive divine oath in the covenant later given to David (see,

---

[11] So McCarthy (*op. cit.*, p. 125; *cf.* p. 170), following M. Cazelles' translation in *La sainte Bible de Jérusalem*.

e.g., II Sam. 7:14ff.; Pss. 89:4[3]; 132:11). And, of course, even if analysis of the data led to the conclusion that the ratificatory procedure for the Deuteronomic Covenant did include a divine oath, the oath of Israel could not be ignored. This covenant would then be based on a bilateral oath, and any claim that the dispensing of this covenant was strictly a matter of divine promise would still be contradicted.

One further example of a covenant that is clearly constituted by Israel's act of commitment will suffice. Joshua 24 describes the renewing of the Lord's covenant with Israel towards the close of Joshua's life. At the climax of the ceremony Israel responded to Joshua's challenge by swearing their allegiance to the Lord their God. The oath sanctions and witnesses are prominent in the account (see verses 15b-24). The covenant-constituting nature of Israel's oath is clearly suggested by the juxtaposition of the final words of that oath (v. 24) and the culminating declaration: "So Joshua made a covenant with the people that day, and set them a statute and an ordinance in Shechem" (v. 25).

The parallelism in Joshua 24:25 between "made a covenant" and "set them a statute and an ordinance" is a plain indication that the biblical author looked on the arrangement thus ratified as a law covenant.[12] That other biblical authors regarded certain divine covenants as having been constituted by human oath of submission to the divinely imposed order of stipulations and sanctions, or, in short, as law covenants, is reflected in the virtual synonymity of "law" and "covenant" in relevant passages. Illustrative of a great volume of biblical evidence for this is the alternating designation of the contents of the two tables of stone as "the ten words (or commandments)" and "the covenant" (*cf.*, *e.g.*, Ex. 34:28; Deut. 4:13; 10:4).[13]

Further confirmation of the existence of a law type of covenant in antiquity and of the identification of the Mosaic and certain other biblical covenants as such law covenants is found in the extra-biblical international vassal treaties and the now familiar parallelism between them and these biblical covenants. A few

---

[12] P. Victor has shown that the word חֹק, "decree" (translated "statute" in Josh. 24:25, *AV*), at times stresses not obligation but privilege (*Vetus Testamentum*, XVI, 3 [July, 1966], 358-361). In Josh. 24, however, the emphasis falls heavily on the demand for Israel's fidelity.

[13] See further Gerhard von Rad, *Old Testament Theology* (New York, 1962), I, 131f. (translation of Vol. I of *Theologie des Alten Testaments* [Munich, 1957]); Eichrodt, *op. cit.*, pp. 54, 63.

scholars, restrained it would seem by an extreme kind of reactionary caution, refuse to follow the obvious direction of the accumulating evidence,[14] but most would agree with the observation of Von Rad: "Comparison of ancient Near Eastern treaties, especially those made by the Hittites in the fourteenth and thirteenth centuries B.C., with passages in the Old Testament has revealed so many things in common between the two, particularly in the matter of form, that there must be some connection between these suzerainty treaties and the exposition of the details of Jahweh's covenant with Israel given in certain passages in the Old Testament."[15]

The Near Eastern vassal treaties were instruments of empire administration. They were law covenants, declarations of the lordship of a great king imposing his authority upon a subject king and servant people. Normally they were ratified by an oath of the vassal, although in some cases the suzerain added his oath, without changing, it need hardly be said, the fundamental law character of the arrangement. To enter into the oath meant for the vassal to come under the dual sanctions of the covenant, the blessing and the curse. The lordship of the great king might be exercised in the form of protection or of destruction. As long as the vassal remained a faithful tributary he might expect to enjoy a relationship of friendship and peace with his suzerain and to receive whatever measure of protection the latter could provide. If, however, the vassal would assert his independence or transfer his allegiance to a new lord he would have to reckon with the vengeance threatened in the treaty against such infidelity and indeed invoked by the vassal himself in his oath of allegiance.

Now since in certain notable instances, particularly but not exclusively in the Mosaic covenants, it pleased the Lord of Israel to describe his covenant relationship to his people according to the pattern of these vassal treaties, no other conclusion is warranted than that "covenant" in these instances denoted *at the formal level* the same kind of relationship as did the vassal covenants on which they were modelled. That is, "covenant" in these divine-human transactions denoted a law covenant and hence

---

[14] A brief account of the situation will be found in the helpful survey article by D. J. McCarthy, "Covenant in the Old Testament: The Present State of Inquiry," *Catholic Biblical Quarterly*, XXVII, 3 (July, 1965), 224f. See, too, the trenchant observations of K. A. Kitchen in *Ancient Orient and Old Testament* (Chicago, 1966), p. 100, n. 51.

[15] *Op. cit.*, p. 132.

was expressive of a lordship that could satisfy the terms of the covenant by stretching forth its sceptre in either blessing or curse.

II. NEW TESTAMENT USAGE

The conclusion towards which all the foregoing points is corroborated by the New Testament evidence. The Pauline usage is particularly pertinent, especially that in the Epistle to the Galatians.

Paul found the difference between two of the Old Testament covenants to be so radical that he felt obliged to defend the thesis that the one did not annul the other (Gal. 3:15ff.). The promise of God to Abraham and his seed (*cf.* Gen. 13:15; 17:8) was not annulled by the law which came later (Gal. 3:17). The chronological details show that Paul was contrasting the promise covenant not to some general law principle but to the particular historical administration of law mediated through Moses at Sinai after Israel's 430 years in Egypt. Incidentally, when Paul speaks of 430 years as the time between promise covenant and law (*cf.* Ex. 12:40ff.; Gen. 15:13), he evidently regards the entire era of the patriarchal triad as the time of the giving of the promise, a perspective found elsewhere, for example, in Psalm 105:9, 10: "*The covenant* which he made with Abraham, and his oath unto Isaac, and confirmed the same unto Jacob for a statute, to Israel for an everlasting covenant" (*ARV*). Significant in this connection is the confirmatory promise in the final revelation of God to Jacob towards the close of the record of the patriarchal period (Gen. 46:2ff., especially v. 4).

The Sinaitic administration, called "covenant" in the Old Testament, Paul interpreted as *in itself* a dispensation of the kingdom inheritance quite opposite in principle to inheritance by guaranteed promise: "For if the inheritance is by law, it is no longer by promise" and "the law is not of faith; but, He that doeth them shall live in them" (Gal. 3:18a, *RSV*, and v. 12, *ARV*; *cf.* Lev. 18:5). Calvin reflects the contrast in principle brought out by Paul when he says that although promises of mercy are found in the law taken as a whole ("the whole law"), they are borrowed elements there and "are not considered as part of the law when the mere nature of the law is the subject of discussion."[16] But, as

---

[16] *Institutes* (English translation by John Allen), II, xi, 7; *cf.* II, ix, 4 and II, xi, 9.

noted above, according to Paul's statements the concept of inheritance by law as over against promise did not find expression merely as a theoretical principle existing problematically within a formal covenant arrangement that was itself promissory, but rather as the governing principle of a particular covenant. Instead of distinguishing between "the whole law" and "the mere nature of the law," therefore, we must distinguish between the entire Mosaic economy, or the total revelation mediated through Moses, and the Sinaitic Covenant as a specific legal whole. And we must recognize that, according to Paul, it was this specific covenantal entity, the Sinaitic Covenant as such, that made inheritance to be by law, not by promise—not by faith, but by works.

How did the apostle arrive at so radical an assessment of the nature of the Sinaitic Covenant as something opposite to promise and faith, an assessment that might seem to jeopardize his great theme of justification by faith alone? He obviously knew that the demands made by God's covenant upon the individual could be construed in a way consistent with the promise principle. For in the theology of Paul the demands of covenant law both as stipulations and sanctions are met and satisfied for men in their faith-identification with the Christ of promise. Indeed, that was the burden of Paul's teaching concerning the law, and he presented it in opposition to those who would construe the law's demands in such isolation from the divine promises that the entire old economy would be reduced to a way of works and so of futility and death. But though Paul as a systematic, or at least biblical, theologian did not view the Sinaitic Covenant in Judaizing isolation from the totality of God's revelation, he was able when it came to historical exegesis to view the Sinaitic Covenant as a separate entity with a character of its own. He did not allow his systematic interests, proper as they were when their turn came, to obscure the radical opposition of the law covenant of Sinai to the principle of inheritance by promise.

But what was there about the Sinaitic Covenant that compelled Paul to identify it so exclusively in terms of law? Elements of redemptive grace were present in and around the transaction. To cite just a feature or two, the historical prologue of the Decalogue-digest of this covenant reminded Israel that the Lord of the covenant was their Redeemer, who had fulfilled ancient promise by leading them forth from bondage; and among the law's sanctions was the promise of mercy, a promise enhanced by the location assigned to the covenant tablets under the mercy seat of the ark of the covenant, a place redolent of atoning grace. Yet Paul identified it as a covenant of law in opposition to promise because there was in his thought, as in that of the Old Testament, a virtual synonymity of covenant and oath, and because the Sinaitic Covenant had been ratified by human oath alone. Promise was present as well as law in this covenant but it was only the law that had been covenantally solemnized. The elements of redemptive promise were not as such formalized by a divine oath of ratification. There was only the human oath, giving covenant form to the law which Israel swore to obey.

In contrast to his classification of the Sinaitic Covenant as law, Paul placed God's covenantal dealings with Abraham in the category of promise, even though they included the ritual of an oath of allegiance sworn by Abraham and his household.[17] For in the course of God's covenant making with Abraham there was another ceremony of covenant ratification, of which we have already taken note, this one involving a divine oath (Gen. 15). It was, moreover, by this ritual of the divine oath that God's covenant relationship to Abraham was first formally established, or (stating it more precisely from the perspective of historical exegesis), that God's relationship to Abraham was first formalized as a covenant. The Sinaitic Covenant, on the other hand, was ratified in the original instance and, indeed, exclusively by the oath of the Israelite vassal; and it was evidently by reason of this difference that Paul identified the Sinaitic Covenant, in radical contrast to the promise given earlier to the patriarchs, as law.

Whatever the explanation, however, the unquestionable fact emerges in Galatians 3 that Paul saw in the Old Testament alongside the covenant of promise another covenant which was so far from being an administration of promise as to raise the urgent question whether it did not abrogate the promise. In the Galatians 3 passage Paul calls only the revelation of promise by the name of "covenant."[18] It would, however, be indefensible to assume that Paul repudiated the propriety of the terminology of the Old Testament according to which that administration of law which Paul here distinguishes so sharply from the covenant of promise was itself known as a "covenant." Moreover, in the fol-

---

[17] *Cf.* Gen. 17. On this, see further Chapter Three.

[18] Elsewhere in the New Testament the term "covenant" is found on occasion as the name of what is distinctly an administration of promise and divine oath; for example, Lk. 1:72, 73; Acts 3:25.

lowing chapter of Galatians Paul himself applies the designation "covenant" to the Sinaitic administration. In Galatians 4:24 Paul says that Sarah and Hagar, according to the allegorical illustration he constructs from their history, "were two covenants." One of these is the Sinaitic Covenant and the other is the covenant of promise, as in the preceding chapter. The contrast between these "two covenants" is, if anything, even more sharply drawn in this passage. The promise covenant is characterized by freedom and the Sinaitic Covenant by bondage. And the thing we are concerned with at present is that in the vocabulary of Paul the Sinaitic administration as such, that is, the administration of law, bondage, condemnation, and death (*cf.* II Cor. 3:6ff.) was a "covenant."

Paul, of course, taught that the Mosaic revelation of law made its contribution within the history of redemption to the fulfillment of the promises (Gal. 3:15ff.). The law covenant did not make the promise covenant of no effect. Somehow the law was administratively compatible with the promise. We have already had to say something about this compatibility, and it will be necessary to say more presently. But even when this compatibility has been affirmed the difference between the two covenants is not denied but rather assumed. The Sinaitic law covenant was consistent with the earlier promise, but as a covenant it did not consist in promise.

Historical exegesis, therefore, contradicts any claim that might be made for the exclusive propriety of the use of "covenant" for divine dispensations of guaranteed promise.[19] The evidence from all sides converges to demonstrate that the systematic theologian possesses ample warrant to speak both of "promise covenant" and, in sharp distinction from that, of "law covenant."

---

[19] "Thus, using only the word ברית itself, that is, employing the method of investigation of terminology, it becomes more and more difficult to write a history of all the ideas which now and then may have made use of it" (Von Rad, *op. cit.*, p. 133).

CHAPTER TWO

LAW COVENANT

There have been some in the history of Covenant Theology, especially in the earliest stage of its development, who have not formulated in specifically covenantal terminology the pre-redemptive special revelation given to Adam as federal head of the race. As we now shift gears from the method of historical exegesis to that of systematic synthesis it is, therefore, first of all to be observed that historical exegesis, by establishing the warrant for speaking of law covenant, invites systematic theology to include the pre-redemptive relationship of God and man within its covenantal formulations.[1]

I. PRE-REDEMPTIVE COVENANT

The mere absence of the word "covenant" from Genesis 1 and 2 does not hinder a systematic formulation of the material of these chapters in covenantal terms, just as the absence of the word "covenant" from the redemptive revelation in the latter part of Genesis 3 does not prevent systematic theology from ana-

[1] It is difficult at best to distinguish between the functions of biblical theology and systematic theology in the treatment of the divine covenants. To analyze these covenants is to trace the history of revelation and divine-human relationship, which is precisely the domain of biblical theology. Certainly, too, biblical theology involves the systematization of the covenantal data under relatively broad historical epochs. The task of systematic theology is hardly distinctive if it consists merely in the summary of the results of biblical theology; and if systematic theology were to de-historicize its treatment of covenant, distilling from the data general truths of divine-human relationship, it would radically misrepresent the object it was defining.

lyzing that passage as the earliest disclosure of the "Covenant of Grace." Obviously the reality denoted by a word may be found in biblical contexts from which that word is absent.[2] So it is in the present case. For the divine administration to Adam at the beginning corresponds fully with the law type of covenant as it appears in the later history. In fact, the biblical theologian discovers that the standard features of ancient law-covenant treaties and administration make most satisfactory categories for the comprehensive analysis of the pertinent data of Genesis 1 and 2. Our claim is not that the literary structure of these opening chapters of Genesis is patterned after the legal form exhibited in the ancient treaties, but simply that the various components of the relationship between God and man found in these chapters correspond to the more significant aspects of the lord-servant relationship attested to by the treaties. In brief, the original relationship of the Creator and man was an administration of God's lordship in the form of a divine protectorate, which God sovereignly established and within which his suzerainty over his human servants was expressed in a revelation of law, including both service obligations and dual sanctions.[3]

There are other biblical perspectives favorable to the formulation of the creation order as covenantal. The postdiluvian ordering of the world revealed in the divine disclosures to Noah (Gen. 8:21–9:17) was in effect a reinstituting of original creation arrangements, and it is designated a "covenant." This administration falls, to be sure, within the era of redemptive history, but it was not itself concerned with the redemptive community as such. Also, though the Noahic Covenant contained certain divine guarantees of blessings, the temporal extension assigned to those very guarantees (*cf.* "while the earth remains," Gen. 8:22) was tantamount to a temporal limitation, and latent in that limitation was the threat of the ultimate vengeance of the covenant Lord against a vassal world that would have despised beyond further divine

[2] Replying to critics of the overall orientation of Old Testament theology to the covenant, Eichrodt observed: "The crucial point is not—as an all too naïve criticism sometimes seems to think—the occurrence or absence of the Hebrew word *b^{e}rît*." The latter was "only the code-word" for something more far-reaching than the word itself (*Theology of the Old Testament*, I, 17f.).

[3] See L. Alonso-Schökel, "Motivos sapienciales y de alianza en Gn 2-3," *Biblica,* 43 (1962), 305-309, for an interesting attempt to trace parallels in technical vocabulary and theme between the Genesis 2 and 3 narrative and covenantal accounts within the subsequent history of salvation.

forbearance the benefits assured to it in this covenant. The close, broad, and basic correspondence between this later order, specifically called a "covenant," and the original order founded by God's work of creation favors a covenantal construction of the latter. To the same effect is the recurring exposition of the covenantal process of salvation as a new work of creation. In Isaiah 43, for example, the history of Israel's election and redemption, the great revelation of God as Yahweh, Lord of the covenant, and the prelude to his formalizing of covenantal relationship with Israel as its King, is described as a creating of Israel. "Thus saith Yahweh, who created thee, O Jacob, and he that formed thee, O Israel (v. 1) . . . I am Yahweh, your Holy One, the creator of Israel, your King" (v. 15). Evidently, Isaiah regarded the Creator's establishment of his kingship over man at the beginning as a prototype of his later covenant making with Israel. Certainly the major elements of the law-covenant structure are present in God's administration of his sovereignty over Adam in Eden. This being so, systematic theology is led by its very nature and purpose as a coordinating and synthesizing science to include the original Edenic administration within its total covenantal framework.

Moreover, the apostle Paul has prepared the way for this step by unifying pre-redemptive and redemptive revelation under the schema of the two Adams. Adam, he tells us, was "the figure" of Christ (Rom. 5:14), meaning that Adam's representative status in God's original government of man is of a piece with the second Adam's representative position in the redemptive administration of the kingdom. Now inasmuch as this position of Christ as representative of his people is inextricably bound up with the administration of the redemptive covenant, it is difficult in the extreme to forbear from construing the position of Adam, "the figure" of Christ, in terms of covenantal arrangement. Romans 5 and I Corinthians 15 are not without their indications of how closely the two-Adams schema and the divine covenants were intertwined in Paul's own thought patterns.

As Paul traces the reign of death from Adam to Christ in Romans 5, he introduces the Mosaic law between those two representative heads, interpreting the law's design as the aggravation of the offense upon which death was the judgment. "Moreover the law entered, that the offense might abound" (v. 20; *cf.* vv. 13, 14). In the covenant context of Galatians 3 there is a significant parallel to this pattern. Once again the law is introduced as occupying an intermediate historical position, this time between the covenant promise to Abraham and its fulfillment in Christ. The purpose of the law, too, is interpreted as in Romans 5:20, such being the force of verse 19: "It was added because of transgressions, till the seed should come to whom the promise was made."

Similarly, I Corinthians 15 is thematically interrelated with Galatians 3 by the subject of kingdom inheritance. The former passage teaches that only those who are in Christ and thus bear the image of the second Adam can inherit the kingdom of God (vv. 42-50). The latter likewise teaches that it is those who are Christ's who are heirs according to the covenant of promise (vv. 18, 29).

Surely it does not become systematic theology to unravel what has been thus synthesized to a degree even in the Scriptures. Systematic theology ought rather to weave together the related biblical strands yet more systematically. Failure to develop the concept of the pre-redemptive covenant as the foundation for redemptive covenant administration will, it may be added, deprive dogmatics of the conceptual apparatus required for a satisfactory synthesis of the work of Christ and the redemptive covenant.

II. THE PRIORITY OF LAW

Once it has been determined that there is law covenant as well as promise covenant and that systematic theology must recognize that the pre-redemptive revelation of law falls within the boundaries of divine covenant administration, we may undertake the construction of a general definition of covenant for use in biblical and systematic theology. This definition must correspond in its formal structure to one of the actual types of arrangement historically called "covenant" and at the same time be serviceable as a unifying formula for the totality of divine-human relationship from creation to consummation. The problem here reduces to the question of the historical, theological, and formal qualifications of law covenant and promise covenant.

Historical priority belongs incontestably to law covenant since pre-redemptive covenant administration was of course strictly law administration without the element of guaranteed, inevitable blessings. By the same token promise covenant is disqualified from the outset as a systematic definition of covenant because it is obviously not comprehensive enough to embrace the pre-redemptive covenantal revelation. It remains, however, to show that law constitutes the ground structure of redemptive covenant administration and thus that a definition of covenant as generically law covenant would be applicable over the whole range of history as is necessary in a systematic theology of the covenant.

This leads us back to the subject of the compatibility of law and promise. Giving a turn to Paul's question whether the covenant of promise was annulled by the subsequent promulgation of a covenant of law, the question of whether the law was against the promises of God, let us now pose the theological issue involved in its earliest historical form: Was the covenant of law established by God at the beginning (Gen. 1 and 2) made of no effect by the subsequent introduction of the promise (Gen. 3:15)? Was the promise against the law of God? No one should hesitate to answer this question, as Paul did his, with a "God forbid." For if there were an annulling of the Edenic law covenant after it had been established by God and later broken by man, then the justice of God would be mutable and his threats vain. God remains just when he justifies the ungodly through his administrations of promise. Herein is the depth of his redemptive wisdom revealed, that in the very process of securing for his chosen the covenant's blessing of life, God honors his original covenant of law in its abiding demand for obedience as the condition of life and with its curse of death for the covenant breakers.

In Romans 3:31 Paul similarly maintains that law is not made void by the promise-faith principle (*cf.* also, Rom. 6). However, it is the regulative character of law as norm of conduct that is in view in Romans 3:31, whereas law in our present discussion is the demand of the justice of God according to which he so declares his righteousness in the salvation of men "that he might be just, and the justifier of him which believeth in Jesus" (Rom. 3:26). Our concern is with law as a principle of inheritance. Moreover, we distinguish between law-inheritance through human works (the inheritance principle as expressed in the Mosaic Covenant viewed as a covenant ratified exclusively by human oath and by which, as Paul affirms, man cannot actually secure the inheritance) and the expression of the law-inheritance principle that centers in the work which Christ, the covenant mediator, performs in declaration of the inherent righteousness of God as he justifies believers.

It is in Christ that the principles of law and promise co-operate unto the salvation of God's people. Ordinary suzerains of antiquity were not able to implement their administrative purposes by sovereign exercises of election, propitiation, and irresistible grace such as would result in the reconciliation and the subsequent perseverance in loyalty of their offending subjects. Consequently, they were unable in their covenants to guarantee to the vassals the perpetuity of those benefits which were contingent on a continuing display of loyalty. But because the Lord of Adam, Abraham, Moses, and Paul is the God of sovereign election and grace, the God who gives Christ as a covenant to his people, he is able to guarantee an everlasting realization of the beatitude of this covenant to his covenant-breaking vassals even while he reaffirms that the fulfillment of the holy demands of his law is the prerequisite of the promised blessings.

Galatians 3:18 must be stressed in Covenant Theology, but so too must Romans 5:18-21. It is by the *obedience* of the one that the many are made righteous unto eternal life. Though the many inherit the blessings not by law (in the Gal. 3:18 sense) but by promise, they are not heirs at all except they are heirs in and through Christ, joint-heirs with Christ. For the promises of the covenant are yea and amen only in Christ. And therefore the promises are made secure to the many according to the principle of inheritance by law after all. For Christ himself enters upon the inheritance as the forerunner, surety, and head of the many only when by his active and passive obedience he has fulfilled the constant *Hauptgebot* of the covenant and submitted to the demand of the curse sanction voiced in the covenant from the beginning. Now if it is the obedience of the one that is the ground of the promise-guarantee given to the many, then clearly the principle of law is more fundamental than that of promise even in a promise covenant.[4]

The difference between pre-redemptive and redemptive covenant is not, then, that the latter substitutes promise for law. The difference could be stated in terms of the substitution of promise for law only if regard were had exclusively for that aspect of redemptive administration dealt with in Galatians 3:18. Offered as

---

[4] All blessings that come to fallen mankind, not exclusively those of salvation, come through Christ and depend on his obedient execution of his Father's will. Common grace belongs within the domain of Christology. Accordingly, the promises of the covenant of Gen. 9, too, involve the principle of blessing contingent on works.

a general or basic analysis of the matter, such a statement of the difference would be deceptively deficient. The difference is rather that redemptive covenant *adds* promise to law. Redemptive covenant is simultaneously a promise administration of guaranteed blessings and a law administration of blessing dependent on obedience, with the latter foundational.

The weakness of the traditional designation, "Covenant of Works," for the pre-redemptive covenant is that it fails to take account of the continuity of the law principle in redemptive revelation and therefore is not a sufficiently distinctive term. The principle of "works" continues into redemptive-covenant administration, not only in the sense already stressed, that the blessings of redemption are secured by the works of a federal head who must satisfy the law's demands, but in the sense, too, that none of the many represented by Christ attains to the promised consummation of the covenant's beatitude unless he attains to that holiness without which man does not see God. With respect to this aspect of the matter the observation is in order that the law's stipulation is compatible with the guarantee of the promise because of the compatibility of human responsibility with the divine sovereignty that is glorified in the immutable decree of election and its irresistible execution by the Holy Spirit.

Furthermore, while the two-Adams schema is not to be divorced from a systematic conception of the covenant, it does not exhaust the latter. Or to put it in other terms, election is not coextensive with redemptive covenant. And the law principle appears in yet another way in the experience of the non-elect within the covenant; for their judgment unto greater condemnation is according to their works, works the more evil because they are in violation of stipulations enhanced by their context of redemptive covenant.

The enunciation of the law principle in the Sinaitic Covenant did not annul the promise given 430 years earlier because this law principle did not come alone or as a substitute for promise. The Sinaitic Covenant in itself, as a covenant ratified by Israel's oath, made law obedience by the Israelites themselves the way of life-inheritance, and yet in the Mosaic revelation as a whole, law was accompanied by promise sealed by divine oath and offering an alternative way of inheritance. Thus the Deuteronomic law covenant mediated through Moses, though not ratified by divine oath in the covenant-making ceremony itself, contained a divine oath sealing the promise of ultimate and eternal restoration of a remnant by the grace of God.[5] Far from being annulled by the covenants mediated through Moses, the promise was renewed in them. And the administrative compatibility of the law and promise principles of inheritance, as joint elements within a single covenant, is explained by the fact that they were alternates to one another.

But our main immediate concern is to observe that even the promise alternate was itself ultimately a way of law—not the way of individual obedience to the law which was explicitly enunciated in the Mosaic covenants, but one which was implicit in the promise itself, the way of vicarious law obedience and satisfaction by the Christ of promise. The Mosaic ritual of atonement gave dramatic symbolic expression to the law basis of the promise, and it is this line of continuity between the Mosaic economy and the New Covenant that is stressed in the book of Hebrews. In the blood of Christ, by which the New Covenant is ratified—for the New Covenant is not ratified by oath ritual, whether performed by men or by God, but rather by a decisive inbreaking of God in an eschatological act of judgment—we witness the faithful fulfillment of the altar promise presented in the old covenants and, by the same token, the inexorable enforcement of the divine law that is basic in all God's covenants.

The conclusion may now be stated that a truly systematic formulation of the theology of the covenant will define covenant generically in the terms of law administration. For there was covenant administration in Eden without the feature of guaranteed promise (*i.e.*, of inevitable and ultimate beatitude), but the principle of inheritance by law has been at the foundation of covenant administration in every age of divine revelation. The Great King of the covenant is unchangeable in his holiness and justice. Merciful he may be according to his sovereign will; but all his works are in righteousness and truth. The satisfaction of the divine law underlies every administration of divine promise.

A systematic definition of covenant in terms of law covenant will have the necessary formal as well as historical and theological qualifications. For law covenant with its duality of sanctions, curse threat as well as offer of blessing, will be formally comprehensive enough to accommodate promise covenant within its generic framework. The addition of the principle of election and guaranteed blessing by which redemptive covenant is distin-

---

[5] Deut. 32:40. *Cf. TGK*, pp. 38f., 132f., and 142ff.

guished from pre-redemptive covenant will not amount to an addition to the formal generic structure, but to a new functional mode for one element (*i.e.*, for the blessing sanction) in the existing law form. This new principle can and must then be treated in the systematic classification of the data not as a generic but as a specific and special covenantal feature.

It is true, as we have seen, that in historical exegesis particular covenants emerge which are in themselves promise covenants (*e.g.*, Gen. 15). Moreover, in systematic formulation we will want to distinguish, within the totality of purpose and achievement that constitute the redemptive covenant, the *proper* purpose of that covenant, namely, the salvation of the elect. But when we recognize this proper soteric purpose we are not to reduce the redemptive covenant to that proper purpose. The mission of Christ offers an analogy, or better, another way of looking at the same thing. The Scriptures declare that the Son of God entered the world to destroy all the works of the Devil (I John 3:8). Surely, too, his coming actually issues in the condemnation of those who believe not (John 3:18). Accordingly, when John 3:17 says that Christ's coming was not to condemn but to save the world, it must be interpreted not as a statement of the total design of the messianic mission but as an indication only of the proper purpose of Christ's coming.

If, then, redemptive covenant is not to be reduced to its proper purpose of grace, much less are we to equate the proper purpose of the redemptive covenant with the generic nature of covenant systematically defined so as to cover both pre-redemptive and redemptive covenant administrations. Unfortunately, Covenant Theology has exhibited a strong bent towards such a reduction of covenant to election. To do so is to substitute a logical abstraction for the historical reality and to shunt systematic theology from its peculiar end of synthetic summation. The covenantal data of historical exegesis which the dogmatic theologian has failed to do justice to in his definition will eventually have to be dealt with somehow or other, but the treatment of them will be problematic and awkward. In fact, it will be impossible to incorporate elements like correlative promise-threat or actual divine vengeance against the disobedient as *covenantal* elements. This impossibility may be obscured by means of a distinction made between an internal and external covenant, but what that manifestly amounts to is the use of the word "covenant" for what is by prior definition the contradiction of covenant.⁶ Other symptoms of the inadequacy of such an approach to the definition of covenant appear in the history of Covenant Theology. Among them are the separation of the so-called "Counsel of Redemption" from the "Covenant of Grace" and not a little of the debate over whether or not the covenant is conditional.

Coherence can be achieved in Covenant Theology only by the subordination of grace to law. Election must be subordinated to covenant, the representative headship of the two Adams to the lordship of God, redemption to creation. Rejection of the equation of covenant with the election-guaranteed promise principle is necessary to avoid the conceptual fragmentation of the theology of the covenant. Covenant conceived of as guaranteed promise cannot assimilate conditional promise. But the covenant concept that has law as its foundation and makes its promises dependent on the obedience of a federal representative can accommodate guaranteed promises. For if the federal representative is the Son of God the prerequisite fulfillment of the law is assured. Moreover, the subordination of grace to law will prove the best way to develop a full-orbed and biblically focused formulation of gospel. For in the broader framework of law covenant Christ's total activity as at once Lord and Servant of the covenant, second Adam and Judge, can be fully integrated in one comprehensive and unified synthesis. And redemption will then be seen for what it is, a two-sided judgment in which the blessing of the covenant comes always through the covenant curse.

⁶ Herman N. Ridderbos' comments on the section of Galatians that has figured in the foregoing discussion may be cited as a recent and typical example (*The Epistle of Paul to the Churches of Galatia* [Grand Rapids, 1953], pp. 130f., n. 2). Ridderbos states that "the essence of the covenant-idea" is the idea of "validity," that is, of "a one-sided grant" or "one-party guarantee." "God's unconditional promise" is the "heart and kernel" of the redemptive covenant. When, therefore, Ridderbos turns to the Sinaitic Covenant with its promises conditioned by stipulations, he must acknowledge that there is "a structural change in the covenant-relationship" and resort to the notion of "a wider and more external meaning" of the covenant in distinction from the covenant as he would define it. But to use the word "covenant" for this external relationship is a *tour de force* after one has committed the fallacy of equating the "covenant-idea" by definition with the proper purpose of redemptive covenant. Ridderbos is more consistent with his own definition when he says: "But, however closely the law is bound up with the promise in the Sinaitic covenant, the fulfillment of the promise is not dependent upon a human fulfillment of the law as attendant condition. *Then God's covenant would no longer be a covenant*" (*ibid.*, pp. 135f.; italics ours).

III. COVENANT AND KINGDOM

If it is recognized that law covenant must provide the formal generic pattern, a systematic definition of covenant may be ventured with assurance that it is at least pointing in the right direction. God's covenant with man may be defined as an administration of God's lordship, consecrating a people to himself under the sanctions of divine law. In more general terms, it is a sovereign administration of the kingdom of God. Covenant administration is kingdom administration. The treaties are the legal instruments by which God's kingship is exercised over his creatures.[7]

Congenial to Reformed theology surely is the centrality of God, the Great King of the covenant, in this definition. It is God's lordship that is the core and constant of the covenant. That covenantal sovereignty of the Lord is manifested in his law, in his imposition of the stipulations of the law and in his infallible declarations respecting the certain execution of the law's dual sanctions, promise and threat. The eventual visitation of either sanction, or of both curse and blessing as in the redemptive judgment that consummates the New Covenant, further reveals the divine lordship and so confirms the covenant.

The theocentric focus of the definition on the divine lordship ought to be continued in the designations for the individual covenantal administrations of the kingdom. The desirability of changing the traditional term, "Covenant of Works," was urged above on the ground that it was not sufficiently distinctive. The other traditional designation, "Covenant of Grace," is also somewhat deficient in the same respect, but not so seriously. Grace, in the specific sense that it effects restoration to the forfeited blessing of God, is of course found only in redemptive revelation. But in another sense grace is present in the pre-redemptive covenant. For the offer of a consummation of man's original beatitude, or rather the entire glory and honor with which God crowned man from the beginning, was a display of the graciousness and goodness of God to this claimless creature of the dust. In addition, as over against the theocentric terms suggested below, the orientation of both the traditional terms is anthropocentric, their concern being with the way in which man attains to the covenant blessings.

The overall unity of the covenants will be provided by the con-

[7] "The *foedus iniquum* of the Sinai covenant, therefore, in fact created a domain with an overlord and subjects; henceforward the idea of the *Kingdom of God* is in the air" (Eichrodt, *op. cit.*, p. 40).

cept of the kingdom of God, of which they are so many manifestations. If a general unifying term were desired it might then be Covenant of the Kingdom. For the two major divisions of the Covenant of the Kingdom our suggestions would be Covenant of Creation and Covenant of Redemption. Since the terms "creation" and "redemption" call attention to God's position in relation to his covenant people as their Maker and Owner-Possessor, they effectively unfold the concept of God's lordship. Moreover, these terms point to a fundamental distinguishing feature of each covenant in the distinctive kind of divine action by which each covenantal order was established.

Inclusion of the idea of consecration in the definition reminds us that the concern of covenant is to establish a special relationship between two parties. At the same time, characterizing this relationship as one of consecration, the consecration of man to God, maintains the theocentric emphasis on the divine sovereignty and glory. It is this absolute sovereignty of God in the reciprocal relationship which, when recognized, prevents the legalistic distortion of the religious-covenantal bond into a mercantile *quid pro quo* contract.[8]

The close association of consecration with law serves to distinguish this law as covenant law. For there is a difference between covenant law and a mere legal code. A law code like Hammurapi's regulates the relationships of the law promulgator's subjects to one another. Covenant law regulates the relationship of the covenant maker's subjects to himself. Covenant law does, to be sure, deal with the mutual relations of the suzerain's vassals but always as an aspect of their allegiance and obligations to the suzerain. The stipulations of the covenant sometimes begin with the declaration of this central and controlling demand for personal allegiance to the overlord; all other additional stipulations are so many specifications of the vassal's primary allegiance. We may point up this fundamental difference between covenant stipulations and ordinary laws by the observation that Moses was not a lawgiver but a covenant mediator.[9] He was not an Israelite

---

[8] *Cf. ibid.*, p. 44.

[9] In the rich mercies of God's covenant with Israel the King of heaven makes this vassal people of the earth his own kingdom proper, as it were. Hence, motifs characteristic of accounts of the relationship of ancient oriental kings to their own people are also found in the total biblical portrayal of God's royal relationship to his earthly subjects. For example, God's reign through Messiah, his Son-King, is depicted as one of establishing

Hammurapi but the agent through whom the Great King of heaven bound a people to himself in a relationship of service. The covenantal commandments revealed through Moses were first and last concerned with the duty of the covenant people to Yahweh their Lord, the duty to walk before him in perfect loyalty.[10]

The mention of consecration also suggests the important oath ritual of the ratification ceremony; it hints, too, at the climactic issue of the covenant in its final consummation to the praise of God. The possible or actual issue of the covenant in a consummation involving both blessing and curse sanctions is not contradicted when covenant is defined in terms of consecration. That is, there is no inconsistency in the combination of consecration and dual sanctions. For the devotion of a doomed Jericho in flames to the satisfaction of God's offended sovereignty is a form of consecration, even if quite different from the consecration of, say, the Nazirites to God's service and favor. Either way man's consecration is the manifestation of God's lordship and so the fulfillment of the covenant.

---

justice for the poor and needy and of being a light to the people, even as the Prologue-Epilogue of Hammurapi's laws claims that he fulfilled the call of the gods to make justice prevail in the land that the strong might not oppress the weak, to rise like the sun over his people and to light the land, and in general to be a savior-shepherd of his people.

[10] The arrangement of the Decalogue with its primary demand to observe Yahweh's exclusive lordship illustrates the peculiarity of covenant law. McCarthy (*Treaty and Covenant*, p. 161) must acknowledge that the Decalogue suits perfectly as the stipulations of a covenant even though he will not grant that the Decalogue exhibits the documentary pattern of ancient treaties. His failure to recognize the treaty form of the Decalogue more fully stems from his acceptance of a fragmenting source analysis of the text which eliminates the sanction formulae from the reconstructed "original" text and otherwise obscures the force of the relevant data from the broader context. It is strange that McCarthy should follow such a method, for, as he is well aware, the kind of interspersing of sanction reminders among stipulations that is found in the Decalogue is attested in a variety of specific ways in many ancient treaties (*cf. ibid.*, pp. 34f., 66, 71, 75). His form-critical study should have led him to abandon the obsolete conclusions of a subjective literary criticism. Instead, he has allowed the pronouncements of literary criticism to warp his interpretation of the objective texts bearing on the Sinai episode and thereby to distort seriously his reconstruction of the history of covenant forms in Israel (*cf. ibid.*, pp. 172ff.).

CHAPTER THREE

CIRCUMCISION: OATH-SIGN OF THE OLD COVENANT

Recent progress in the recovery of the detailed form of ancient Near Eastern covenant ceremony calls for a fresh study of the corresponding covenant rituals of Israel and of the New Testament church. Perhaps, re-examined in a more authentic historical context, these familiar symbols of our religious life may break through their traditional incrustations and emerge in something closer to their pristine shape and significance. Our concern in the investigation that follows will be particularly with the rites of circumcision and baptism, the signs employed in connection with incorporation into the covenant community, old and new.

I. MALEDICTION

Genesis 17 contains the record of the institution of circumcision as a sign of God's covenant with Abraham and his house. This chapter is not, like the Decalogue or Deuteronomy, the text of a treaty but an historical narrative describing the ratification ceremony of the covenant. The narrative, however, consists largely of the words that God spoke to Abraham on that occasion, and those words comprise the standard elements found in ancient vassal treaties.[1] Although the account in Genesis 17 does not include the customary historical prologue, the somewhat earlier

---

[1] In his doctoral dissertation, *Zur Datierung der "Genesis-P-Stücke"* (Kampen, 1964), Samuel R. Külling argues from the treaty pattern in Genesis 17 to the unity and early date of the chapter. He indicates the wider implications of his conclusions for documentary theories that regard Genesis 17 as part of the supposed P-source. On the treaty pattern generally see *TGK*.

covenant revelation to Abraham recorded in Genesis 15 contains a Decalogue-like combination of titulature and history: "I am the Lord that brought thee out of Ur of the Chaldees" (v. 7).[2] Only if the unity of Genesis were first destroyed by a divisive source criticism could the partial incompleteness[3] of the treaty pattern in Genesis 17 be urged with any plausibility at all as grounds for hesitation in identifying this transaction with the international treaty form.

Corresponding to the usual preamble with its introduction of the speaker is the Lord's declaration to Abraham: "I am God Almighty" (v. 1b). Prominently featured are the stipulations of this covenant, including the so-called *Grundsatzerklärung*, a general statement of the nature of the covenantal relationship: Yahweh will be a God to Abraham and his descendants (v. 7) and Abraham is to walk before him in true loyalty (v. 1c). The special obligation laid upon the covenant servants is that of circumcision (vv. 9-14). The communal performance of this rite on that very day served to consummate the ratificatory proceedings of this particular covenantal engagement (vv. 23-27). But the obligation of circumcision was to continue beyond that day as a permanent duty of the Abrahamic community. Certain specific obligations are assumed by the Lord of the covenant also, as is the case in some of the extra-biblical treaties, though rarely. These are appropriately expressed in the form of promises (vv. 2, 4-8). Since in this covenant the Suzerain is also the divine Witness, the promissory obligations which Yahweh undertakes as Suzerain are also a blessing sanction which he will honor as the divine Witness when he beholds faithfulness in the covenant servant. Another element of the treaty pattern, *viz.*, the sanctions, is thus included here among the stipulations.[4] Curse sanction appears too, appended to the stipulation regarding circumcision (v. 14). Also in the category of divine promise or blessing sanction is the further revelation centering in the role of Sarah (vv. 15-21).

[2] *Cf.* Josh. 24:2ff. for another version of this in a later historical prologue.

[3] The absence of the historical prologue would not constitute incompleteness according to the analysis of McCarthy, who maintains that this historical section was not indispensable even in second-millennium treaties. See his *Treaty and Covenant*, pp. 30, 31 and his discussion in *The Catholic Biblical Quarterly*, XXVII, 3 (July, 1965), 227ff., especially n. 23. But *cf.* further Kitchen, *Ancient Orient and Old Testament*, pp. 93-95.

[4] See above, Chapter Two, n. 10.

In short, the transaction recorded in Genesis 17 may be identified as a covenant of the vassal type, an administration of the lordship of the covenant Giver, binding his servant to himself in consecrated service under dual sanctions, blessing and curse.

Attention has already been called to the special importance of the oath in the establishment of the international treaties. In parity covenants the ratificatory oath was taken by both parties, but in other covenants the sworn commitment was ordinarily unilateral. It was by an oath that the vassal expressed his incorporation within the sphere of the lord's jurisdiction. This oath invoked the covenant sanctions, more precisely, the curse, so that curse became a synonym for oath. And this oath-curse was customarily dramatized in symbolic rites, the ritual actions portraying the doom that was verbally specified in the self-maledictory oath.[5] An interesting example of such an oath-rite is found in the eighth-century treaty of Ashurnirari V and Mati'ilu:

> This ram is not brought from his herd for sacrifice, nor is he brought out for a *garitu*-festival, nor is he brought out for a *kinitu*-festival, nor is he brought out for (a rite for) a sick man, nor is he brought out for slaughter a[s. . . .] It is to make the treaty of Ashurnirari, King of Assyria, with Mati'ilu that he is brought out. If Mati'ilu [sins] against the treaty sworn by the gods, just as this ram is broug[ht here] from his herd and to his herd will not return [*and stand*] at its head, so may Mati'ilu with his sons, [his nobles,] the people of his land [be brought] far from his land and to his land not return [*to stand*] at the head of his land.
>
> This head is not the head of a ram; it is the head of Mati'ilu, the head of his sons, his nobles, the people of his land. If those named [sin] against this treaty, as the head of this ram is c[ut off,] his leg put in his mouth [. . .] so may the head of those named be cut off [. . . .] This shoulder is not the shoulder of a ram, it is the shoulder of the one named, it is the shoulder of [his sons, his nobles], the people of his land. If Mati'ilu sins against this treaty, as the shou[lder of this ram] is torn out, [. . .] so may the [shoulder of the one na]med, [his] sons, [his nobles,] the people of [his land] be torn out [. . .] (col. 1:10ff.).[6]

Oath-curse was, moreover, practically synonymous with cove-

---

[5] Some of the similes used in prophetic threats of judgment in the Old Testament are found to reflect the formulae recited at these substitution rites depicting the curses of the covenant oath. *Cf.* Hillers, *Treaty-Curses and the Old Testament Prophets*, pp. 19ff.

[6] The translation is that given in McCarthy, *Treaty and Covenant*, p. 195.

nant (*cf., e.g.,* Deut. 29:11 [12]) and the substitution rites symbolizing the oath-curse coalesced with the rites which ratified the covenant. In the treaty just cited, for example, it is the ram which is brought out for the explicit purpose of making the treaty that serves at the same time expressly to represent the vassal people suffering the curse of the oath of allegiance sworn by Mati'ilu. The ram cut off from the herd never to return, the ram with its head and other members severed, symbolized the curse fate of the covenant breaker. But it was this same cutting off of the ram that made the covenant.[7] The practice of slaying an animal in the ceremony of covenant ratification is widely attested,[8] and out of this common rite arose the familiar biblical and extra-biblical terminology of "cutting a covenant" and the synonymous "cutting a curse."[9]

It is generally recognized that a dismembering ritual like that described in Genesis 15 is to be explained by reference to the complex of concepts and ceremonies we have just described.[10] But here, too, is the historical-juridical context for the understanding of the vassal covenant of Genesis 17 and, more particularly, for the interpretation of its cutting-off rite of circumcision. This means that circumcision was the rite by which the covenant of Genesis 17 was "cut." It means further that circumcision symbolized the oath-curse by which the Abrahamic community confessed themselves under the judicial authority and more precisely under the sword of God Almighty.[11]

[7] McCarthy (*op. cit.,* pp. 55ff.) rightly rejects the interpretation that sees in the cutting up of an animal to make a covenant the idea of an association of life effected through the mystic force of the sacrificial blood. He defends the common view that the ceremony is a *Drohritus,* an enacted curse threat against the swearer of the oath lest he dare violate it.

[8] The kind of animal used varied; sheep, ass, and pig are among those mentioned in extra-biblical texts. For a discussion of covenant ceremonies, including Greek and Roman, which involved a young animal and an herb, and of the possible relevance of this for the Hebrew Passover lamb and hyssop, see G. E. Mendenhall, "Puppy and Lettuce in Northwest-Semitic Covenant Making," *Bulletin of the American Schools of Oriental Research,* 133 (Feb., 1954), 26-30. *Cf.* F. C. Fensham, "Did a Treaty Between the Israelites and Kenites Exist?", *Bulletin of the American Schools of Oriental Research,* 175 (Oct., 1964), 51-54.

[9] See Gen. 15:9ff., 18; Jer. 34:18. *Cf.* McCarthy, *op. cit.,* pp. 53ff., and Hillers, *op. cit.,* p. 20, n. 27.

[10] See further below and *cf.* above, Chapter One, pp. 16f.

[11] *Cf.* Josh. 5:13; Rom. 13:4; Rev. 19:15, 16. The Joshua 5 theophany account follows the record of the circumcising of the generation of the

What is suggested by the broad structure of Genesis 17 is confirmed by the particulars about circumcision given in verses 9-14. Circumcision is called God's covenant, his covenant in the flesh of his people (vv. 9, 10, 13). This identification of covenant with circumcision reminds us at once of the coalescence of the covenant with its oath-curse in the extra-biblical treaties. Moreover, the meaning of circumcision as symbol of the oath-curse is actually expressed in so many words in verse 14. There the threat of the curse sanction sounds against the one who breaks the covenant by not obeying the command of circumcision: "(he) shall be cut off." The use of the verb *kārat* in this specific description of the curse clearly echoes the idiom of cutting a covenant (*kārat b^{e}rît*), and it is an unmistakable allusion to the nature of the rite of circumcision. So in this, the primary passage for the interpretation of circumcision, the general and specific considerations unitedly point to the conclusion that circumcision was the sign of the oath-curse of the covenant ratification. In the cutting off of the foreskin the judgment of excision from the covenant relationship was symbolized.[12]

II. CONSECRATION

The oath whose curse sanction circumcision symbolized was an oath of allegiance. It was an avowal of Yahweh as covenant Lord, a commitment in loyalty to him. As the symbolized curse which sealed this pledge of allegiance, circumcision partook of the import of the oath. It was, therefore, a sign of consecration. Hence Israel is commanded: "Circumcise yourselves to the Lord" (Jer. 4:4).

---

wilderness wandering (Josh. 5:2ff.). It is as if the sword of the captain of the host of the Lord had been turned away from the uncircumcised nation by their cutting the covenant-allegiance oath anew through circumcision, and only then could be directed against the Canaanites to cut them off from the land. *Cf.* Ezek. 28:10; 31:18; 32:10ff. for the association of the death of the uncircumcised with that of the victim of the sword. On this usage in Ezekiel, *cf.* O. Eissfeldt, "Schwerterschlagene bei Hesekiel" in *Studies in Old Testament Prophecy*, ed. H. H. Rowley (New York, 1950), pp. 73-81. *Cf.*, too, the cutting-off curse of the hypocrite in 1QS, II, 16, 17, and the appeal made to it by O. Betz to interpret Matt. 24:51 and Acts 1:18 in "The Dichotomized Servant and the End of Judas Iscariot," *Revue de Qumran*, 17, 5 (Oct., 1964), 43-58.

[12] A more precise analysis of the implications of the circumcision of the foreskin for the curse significance of circumcision will be found below in Chapter Six.

Circumcision's consecratory import appears in the figurative use made of the idea in the law of the fruit trees in Leviticus 19:23-25. For the first three years the fruit was regarded as "uncircumcised" and might not be eaten. The fruit of the fourth year was to be consecrated in joyful praise to the Lord, and then Israel might eat of the fruit of the fifth year.[13] According to this pattern it was the act of consecrating the tree in its firstfruit to the Lord that terminated the state of uncircumcision and so constituted the circumcision of the tree.

For Abraham the consecratory purpose of circumcision was brought home in another cutting ritual he was afterwards required to perform. When Isaac the son of promise was born, Abraham had circumcised him on the eighth day as God had commanded (Gen. 21:4). But later God summoned Abraham to take up the knife again and to perfect Isaac's circumcision by cutting him off altogether from among the living (Gen. 22:1ff.). The identification of this cutting off of Isaac as "a burnt offering" (v. 2), the form of sacrifice expressive of total consecration, illuminates the meaning of these knife rituals. Circumcision, whether partial or complete, was an act of consecration.

With this demand laid upon Abraham to perfect the circumcision of his son, he was confronted with the dilemma of circumcision-consecration. The son of Adam who would consecrate himself to God in the obedience of covenant service can do so only by passing through the judgment curse which circumcision symbolizes. Isaac must be cut off in death at the altar of God. In the circumcision of the foreskin on the eighth day he had passed under the judgment knife of God apart from God's altar in a merely symbolic, token act of conditional malediction. But this cutting off of the whole body of Isaac's flesh to be consumed in the fire of the altar of God was a falling under the actual judgment curse. This was an infliction in reality of that curse which was but symbolized by the ordinary circumcision made with hands. How then can there be a realization of the proper purpose of the redemptive covenant administered to Abraham? How can Isaac be consecrated to living service in the favor of God if he must be consecrated in death as an object of divine condemnation? And how can there be a fulfillment of the decree of election

---

[13] Law 60 of the Code of Hammurapi also specifies the fifth year as that in which the produce of the orchard began to be shared by the owner and gardener.

if the whole redemptive program aborts here and now in the damnation of Isaac?

The answer to this dilemma began to unfold in an earlier knife rite, or circumcision, in which Abraham had participated. Genesis 15 tells us of a covenant cutting and a theophany which Abraham witnessed amid darkness and horror—the only proper setting for this Old Testament Golgotha. There in the passage of God, in the divided theophanic symbol of smoking furnace and flaming torch, between the dismembered creatures the mystery of the abandonment of the Son of God emerged beforehand. For what Abraham witnessed was the strange self-malediction of the Lord of the covenant, who would himself undergo the covenant's curse of cutting asunder rather than fail to lead his servant into the promised fulness of beatitude.

From this knife ceremony Abraham might later elicit the meaning of the cutting rite which God appointed to him as the sign of the covenant in his flesh. And remembering this same divine oath-curse of dismembering, Abraham on the mount of Moriah might more fully comprehend what it meant that God had stayed the knife of judgment in his hand and had showed him Isaac's substitute caught by its horns in the thicket. When the hour of darkness should come, it was the Lord who would himself be Isaac's sacrificial ram. What God had before declared himself ready to do in order to fulfill the covenant promise to Abraham, he now by the ram intimates that he will do—he will himself come under the judgment knife and suffer the curse as a substitute for sinners.

Read together in the light of fulfillment, the three cutting rituals of Genesis 15, 17, and 22 proclaim the mystery of a divine circumcision—the circumcision of God in the crucifixion of his only-begotten. Paul called it "the circumcision of Christ" (Col. 3:11). The circumcision of the infant Jesus in obedience to Genesis 17, that partial and symbolic cutting off, corresponded to the ritual of Genesis 15 as a passing of one who was divine under the curse threat of the covenant oath. That was the moment, prophetically chosen, to name him "Jesus." But it was the circumcision of Christ in crucifixion that answered to the burnt-offering of Genesis 22 as a perfecting of circumcision, a "putting off" not merely of a token part but "of the [whole] body of the flesh" (Col. 2:11, ARV), not simply a symbolic oath-cursing but a cutting off of "the body of his flesh through death" (Col. 1:22) in accursed darkness and dereliction.

Here, then, was the direction for faith to look for the solution to the dilemma of circumcision as a sign of consecration. By the demand to slay Isaac, God reminds us that all the ordinary generation of Adam, even Abraham and his promised seed, are covenant breakers and must be consecrated to him by coming to the place of the curse. But beholding the ram on Moriah and God's own oath ritual of dismembering, may not even Old Testament faith have discerned the way of grace, the way of identification with God in his cutting off in the dread darkness, the way that cannot but lead through the curse into blessing, beyond death unto life?[14] The prophet who later wrote of the messianic Servant that "he was cut off out of the land of the living, stricken for the transgression of my people" (Isa. 53:8b, RSV) might have articulated this Old Testament identification faith in some such assurance to the faithful as this: You were cut off with the Servant in circumcision, wherein also you were buried with him, whose grave is appointed with the wicked, and you were also raised with him, for he shall be exalted and divide the spoil with the strong.

That, in any case, is the gospel of circumcision according to Paul. In the Colossians 2 passage already cited Paul affirms the union of the Christian with Christ in his crucifixion-circumcision: "in whom ye were also circumcised with a circumcision not made with hands, in the putting off of the body of the flesh, in the circumcision of Christ; having been buried with him in baptism, wherein ye were also raised with him through faith in the working of God, who raised him from the dead" (vv. 11, 12, ARV). That Paul here interprets circumcision as a dying or death is clear from the sequence of ideas: circumcision, burial, resurrection (*cf.* Rom. 6:3, 4). This is confirmed by the exposition of circumcision as a "putting (or stripping) off,"[15] the latter being in turn synonymous with "putting to death" (Col. 3:5-9).[16] As a death in union with Christ, the representative sin-bearer, in his crucifixion, the Christian's circumcision-death is an undergoing of the wrath of God against sin, a falling under his sword of judgment. It is a

[14] *Cf.* Heb. 11:19.

[15] The noun ἀπέκδυσις, "removal, stripping off," is used in Col. 2:11 and the verb ἀπεκδύομαι in Col. 2:15. The noun is found only here in Scripture and elsewhere only in dependence on Paul. The verb is found only here and in Col. 3:9, which is, therefore, to be regarded as a further exposition of circumcision.

[16] For the equivalence with "crucifying" see also Rom. 6:6; Gal. 2:20; 5:24; 6:12-15.

judicial death as the penalty for sin.[17] Yet, to be united with Christ in his death is also to be raised with him whom death could not hold in his resurrection unto justification. So it is that circumcision, which in itself as a symbolic action signifies the sword of the Lord cutting off his false servants, as a sign of the Covenant of Redemption takes on, alongside the import of condemnation, that of justification, the blessing that may come through the curse.

Paul traces this wider import of circumcision beyond justification so as to include regeneration and sanctification. The appropriate expression and inevitable accompaniment of our judicial circumcision-death in Christ is the death of the old man, our dying to the dominion of sin. Paul interprets the circumcision–putting off as such a spiritual transformation, if not in Colossians 2:11bff.,[18] yet clearly so in Colossians 3:5-9. The element of subjective, spiritual-moral qualification thus occupies a place in the Pauline doctrine of circumcision as a derivative from the rite's prior meaning as a sign of the objective curse of the covenant.

Elsewhere, too, in both the Old and New Testaments the idea appears in the form of demand, declaration, and promise that when the consecration sworn in the circumcision oath is fulfilled in the power of the redemptive principle operative in the covenant, it becomes a matter of heart-consecration in the obedience of love to the covenant Lord. A specific, spiritualized usage developed according to which the redemptively consecrated heart and various other organs of expression for such a heart, like the lips and ears, were spoken of as circumcised. In fact, as touching the righteousness of the law (or the proper purpose of the covenant) Paul warned that the circumcision of the flesh without circumcision of the heart was uncircumcision (Rom. 2:25-29; *cf.* Lev. 26:41; Deut. 10:16; 30:6; Jer. 4:4; 6:10; 9:24, 25 [25, 26]; Acts 7:51; Rom. 4:11; Phil. 3:3).

Conclusions: The theology of circumcision can be summarized in the ideas of malediction, consecration, identification, justification, and spiritual qualification. The ancient rituals of covenant ratification, both biblical and their international parallels, provide the original historical setting for the interpretation of this ordinance. In this light circumcision is found to be an oath-rite

---

[17] Note Paul's juridical development of his theme in Col. 2:13ff.

[18] For a further discussion of the exegesis of this passage see below in Chapter Five under "Baptism as Ordeal."

and, as such, a pledge of consecration and a symbol of malediction. That is its primary, symbolic significance.

Beyond that, the broader import of circumcision is determined by the specific nature of that covenant of which it is declared to be a sign, and especially, since circumcision is a sanction sign, by the peculiar nature of the judgment in which that covenant issues. As for the covenant, it was a law covenant, not a simple guarantee of blessing but an administration of the lordship of God, a covenant therefore which confronted the servant with dual sanctions, curse and blessing. And the carrying out of the sanctions in these oath-ratified covenants was regarded as the rendering of a direct verdict by the God (gods) of the oath, that is, as a trial by ordeal.[19]

Hence, by circumcision, the sign of the consecratory oath of the Abrahamic Covenant, a man confessed himself to be under the juridical authority of Yahweh and consigned himself to the ordeal of his Lord's judgment for the final verdict on his life. The sign of circumcision thus pointed to the eschatological judicial ordeal with its awful sanctions of eternal weal or woe.

In the case of a covenant with the fallen sons of Adam, their nature as covenant breakers from their youth would seem to preclude any outcome for the divine ordeal other than condemnation. Yet the very fact that God makes a covenant with such subjects reveals that along with justice the principle of redemptive grace is operative here with its totally new and unpredictable possibilities. The covenant is a law covenant but it is a redemptive law covenant. Accordingly, its consummating judgment is a redemptive judgment, the curse of which can be suffered not only (not even properly) by the covenant servant in himself; it may also be undergone by him in the divine Redeemer-Substitute. In the one case the curse is curse and no more; in the other, the curse becomes the way to beatitude. Redemptive judgment thus consists in an execution of the covenant's dual sanctions in the

---

[19] According to the ideology of the international treaties the covenant relationship had a religious basis, being established under the sanctions of the gods. Hence the military engagement occasioned by the violation of the treaty was a trial by ordeal, a judgment of the oath deities. Note, for example, in the Tukulti-Ninurta historical epic the account of the victory of the Assyrians over the Babylonians in consequence of the offenses of the Babylonian king, Kashtiliash, and of the siding of all the gods with Tukulti-Ninurta. See further, McCarthy, *op. cit.*, pp. 92f.

form of curse and blessing-through-curse.[20] This, therefore, is what circumcision signifies. The original maledictory meaning of circumcision continues throughout the broad spectrum of its meaning, curse being an integral, if penultimate, element even in the judgment of the blessed.

"And it shall come to pass, that in all the land, saith the Lord, two parts therein shall be cut off and die; but the third shall be left therein" (Zech. 13:8). Here the potential symbolized in circumcision is prophetically viewed in its historical actualization as the prophet interprets the future of the covenant as a fulfillment of the malediction invoked at its beginning.

Judgment will befall the covenant community, a time of cutting off. For two-thirds the circumcision-judgment will be unto death. But a third part will be left in whom the consecration pledged in circumcision will be realized according to the proper purpose of redemptive covenant. Of them the Lord says, "It is my people"; and they respond, "The Lord is my God" (v. 9b). Even this destiny, however, is reached only by a passage of this remnant "through the fire" (v. 9a); they, too, must undergo the ordeal symbolized by circumcision. And Zechariah penetrates yet deeper into the mystery of circumcision when he speaks of God's judgment sword wielded against a God-man: "Awake, O sword, against my shepherd, and against the man that is my fellow, saith the Lord of hosts: smite the shepherd, and the sheep shall be scattered: and I will turn mine hand upon the little ones" (v. 7). Here Old Testament prophecy proclaims the New Testament's deliverance out of the malediction of human circumcision by pointing to the malediction-benediction of the circumcision-resurrection of Christ.[21]

---

[20] The blessing is attained through the curse suffered by Christ, but it is also true that the blessing is a resultant of Christ's infliction of the curse on the enemies of the blessed. That is the principle expressed in the eschatological concept of the final decisive conflict between the saints and the Satanic hordes.

[21] *Cf.* Matt. 26:31, 32; Mk. 14:27, 28.

CHAPTER FOUR

JOHN'S BAPTISMAL SIGN OF JUDGMENT

In view of the conclusions we have reached concerning circumcision we are bound to ask ourselves whether traditional approaches to Christian baptism may not have unduly restricted its import too. According to Reformed theology, baptism is a sacramental seal of the benefits of Christ's grace, a sign of union with the triune God and of those judicial and spiritual blessings that are secured in Christ. But this theology, appealing (rightly) to the unity of the divine covenants, has maintained that the significance of baptism corresponds to that of circumcision. Does, then, the New Testament encourage or even clearly require us to interpret baptism, not exclusively as a sign of blessing, but, like circumcision, as a sign of Christ's redemptive judgment with its benedictions and maledictions alike? Must we enlarge our theology of baptism so as to see in it a more comprehensive symbol of the eschatological judgment that consummates the covenant of which baptism is a sign?[1]

What follows by way of an account of Johannine baptism in this chapter and of Christian baptism in the next is not presented as a general survey of New Testament teaching on the subject. The emphasis will be one-sided because our purpose is simply to

---

[1] See C. F. D. Moule, "The Judgment Theme in the Sacraments" in *The Background of the New Testament and Its Eschatology* (C. H. Dodd Festschrift), ed. W. D. Davies and D. Daube (Cambridge, 1956), pp. 464-481. Moule develops the thesis that the New Testament regards baptism and holy communion as anticipations of the last judgment.

call attention to what we believe to be a neglected element in the meaning of this ordinance of Christ. Although silence is not then to be construed necessarily as rejection of other aspects of the matter, it may be acknowledged at once that the incorporation of the new element would seem to require a change in the total bearing and the central thrust of the traditional doctrine of baptism.

I. MESSENGER OF ULTIMATUM

However the precise relationship between the baptism administered by John the Forerunner and that of the Christian church is to be defined, the significance of the earlier rite naturally entered into the apostolic conception of baptism as ordained for them by the Lord Jesus. John indeed compared his ministry and that of Jesus explicitly in terms of baptism (Matt. 3:11, 12). It is, therefore, important to observe that in the revelation associated with John, baptism is emphatically a sign of eschatological judgment.

In order to see the mission of John the Forerunner in proper historical perspective it will be useful to review certain procedures followed in ancient covenant administration. Of special interest at this point is the institution of the covenant lawsuit, which is currently attracting considerable notice among Old Testament scholars, particularly because of the contribution it makes to our understanding of the historical function of the prophets and to the form-critical analysis of their messages. When a vassal failed to satisfy the obligations of the sworn treaty, the suzerain instituted a covenant lawsuit against him. The legal process was conducted by messengers. In the first of its two distinct phases messengers delivered one or more warnings. These were couched in a form that reflected the pattern of the original treaty. Stylistically, interrogation was a distinctive feature. The vassal was reminded of the suzerain's benefits and of the treaty stipulations, explanation of his offenses was demanded, and he was admonished to mend his ways. He was also confronted anew with the curses of the covenant, now in the form of an ultimatum, and warned of the vanity of all hope of escape through recourse to any alien quarter. If the messenger of the great king was rejected, imprisoned, and especially if he was killed, the legal process moved into its next phase. This was the declaration of war as an execution of the sacred sanctions of the treaty, and so as a visitation of the oath deities against the offender, a trial by ordeal.[2]

The mission of the Old Testament prophets, those messengers of Yahweh to enforce the covenant mediated to Israel through Moses, is surely to be understood within the judicial framework of the covenant lawsuit. So too the mission of John the Baptist. John was sent with the word of ultimatum from Yahweh to his covenant-violating vassal, Israel.

Was it not precisely this judicial process that Jesus had in mind when he interpreted the succession of divine messengers in the parable of the vineyard (Matt. 21:33ff.; Mk. 12:1ff.; Lk. 20:9ff.)? The servants of the parable were sent by the "lord of the vineyard" to demand for him his due. But the husbandmen repudiated their obligations, handled the messengers shamefully, beat them, stoned them, sent them away empty, even killed some of them. That the rejection of John was particularly in view in this parable is indicated by its location immediately after the record of Jesus' counter-challenge to the Jewish authorities with respect to the origin of John's baptism (*cf.* Matt. 21:23-32; Mk. 11:27-33; Lk. 20:1-8). And Jesus himself was of course the lord of the vineyard's son, who was cast out and slain. Because Israel had repudiated his lordship and despised his ultimatum, God would inflict on them the vengeance of the covenant.[3] In fact, Jesus, as the final

---

[2] On this legal process see Julien Harvey, "Le 'Rîb-Pattern', réquisitoire prophétique sur la rupture de l'alliance," *Biblica*, 43, 2 (1962), 172-196. *Cf.* my *TGK*, p. 139. Since the ways of the gods were portrayed after human analogues, it is not surprising to find evidence of such legal procedure in mythological texts as well as in historical-legal documents. There is, for example, the episode in the Ugaritic epic of Baal (Gordon, *UH*, 137) where the god Yamm sends his messenger-witnesses (*mlak ym t'dt tpt nhr*) with an ultimatum to the assembly of the gods. The messengers address them in the name of Yamm, "your lord" and "your master" (*b'lkm adnkm*), while the terror-stricken gods are acknowledged by El as "thy tributaries" (*mnḫyk*) and Yamm is promised his "tribute" (*argmn;* compare the use of this term in the account of Niqmad's tribute to his Hittite suzerain, Shuppiluliuma, in Gordon, *UH*, 118:18, 24). Significantly, it is narrated that Baal was on the verge of slaying the messengers. Such a rejection of the ultimatum would have challenged Yamm to enter the second stage of his lawsuit. And, of course, as it falls out, the case is determined in a trial by ordeal through individual combat, Baal vanquishing the Sea-dragon and securing for himself the eternal dominion.

[3] For supplementation of the announcement of destruction, see the parable of the marriage of the king's son, which follows immediately in Matthew (22:2ff.).

messenger of the covenant, was declaring the verdict against Israel in the very process of speaking unto them this parable.

It is possible to discern reflections of the ancient covenant lawsuit paradigm in these words of Jesus. Parabolic though it is in form, this discourse was part of a legal conflict of Jesus with the officialdom of Israel over the precise subject of covenant authority (*cf.* Matt. 21:23; Mk. 11:28; Lk. 20:2). The parable served to remind them of the benefits bestowed by the Lord of the covenant: he had planted the vineyard, hedged it about, dug the winepress, and built the tower. The parable also confronted the vassals with the treaty stipulations and their disloyalty in failing to present their tribute at the appointed season. Nor is the interrogative element missing; it was by a question that Jesus elicited from the recalcitrants themselves their own verdict of destruction and disinheritance (*cf.* Matt. 21:40, 41). And the whole discourse issued in a solemn decree of judgment (*cf.* Matt. 21:42f.; Mk. 12:10f.; Lk. 20:17f.). Similarly, the song of the vineyard in Isaiah 5:1ff., on which our Lord's parable is an evident variation, is structured according to the pattern of the covenant lawsuit. The judicial character of the song is plainly indicated by Yahweh's summons: "And now, O inhabitants of Jerusalem, and men of Judah, judge, I pray you, betwixt me and my vineyard" (v. 3). The parallel between this song and Jesus' parable thus penetrates beyond the common figure of the vineyard to a common covenantal crisis and judicial process.

To the same effect as Jesus' parable of the vineyard had been Malachi's prophetic interpretation of the coming Lord and his Forerunner; he, too, depicted them as the bearers of the ultimatum and the final verdict. For Malachi spoke of two messengers, the one called "my [*i.e.*, the Lord's] messenger" and the other, "the messenger of the covenant" (Mal. 3:1). Of the first he wrote: "he shall prepare the way before me."[4] Again, Malachi spoke of

---

[4] A similar figure is used in the Nimrud treaty of Esarhaddon to describe the vassal's obligation to accept the lordship of the crown prince Ashurbanipal when the time of his accession to the throne had come: "You will set a fair path at his feet" (line 54, translation of D. J. Wiseman in *The Vassal-Treaties of Esarhaddon* [London, 1958], p. 34). The same demand expressed in the same imagery was attributed by Isaiah (40:3) to the voice that should cry in the wilderness, the voice with which John identified himself (Jn. 1:23; *cf.* Matt. 3:3; Mk. 1:3; Lk. 3:4). On the use and importance of Isa. 40:3 in the Qumran community (*cf.* 1QS, VIII, 13, 14) see W. H. Brownlee, *The Meaning of the Qumran Scrolls for the Bible* (New York, 1964), pp. 83ff., 110ff.

a coming of "Elijah" (*i.e.*, John; *cf.* Matt. 11:14; 17:12f.; Mk. 9:12f.; Lk. 1:17) as a precursor of "the great and terrible day of the Lord." His mission was to be one of warning lest Israel's Lord smite them "with a curse" (Mal. 3:23, 24 [4:5, 6]). For at his fiery advent the Lord would refine his people by judgment (*cf.* Mal. 3:2ff.).[5]

What is narrated in the Gospels concerning the ministry of John comports fully with the understanding of his role as that of messenger of the covenant to declare the Lord's ultimatum of eschatological judgment. The voice in the wilderness cried, "Repent ye: for the kingdom of heaven is at hand" (Matt. 3:2). It warned of "the wrath to come" and of the vanity of reliance on external earthly relationships, even descent from Abraham. If the trees did not bring forth satisfactory fruit, if they were not properly circumcised unto the Lord (*cf.* Lev. 19:23-25), then they must be cursed as a cumbrance to the ground and cut off. The axe was even now "laid unto the root" to inflict this judgment of circumcision (*cf.* Matt. 3:7ff.; Lk. 3:7ff.).

One would expect that the baptism of John as the sign of such a mission of ultimatum would portray by its own symbolic form the threatened ordeal of divine judgment. Of course, in the usually alleged ritual antecedents of John's baptism (*viz.*, the Levitical lustrations, proselyte baptism, the Qumran washings) and frequently in the figurative use of water in the prophets[6] it is the cleansing property of water that is in view. Moreover, John's baptism is called a "baptism of repentance unto the remission of sins" (Mk. 1:4; Lk. 3:3, *ARV*). Consequently, the baptismal waters of John have been understood as symbolic of a washing away of the uncleanness of sin. But the possibility must be probed whether this water rite did not dramatize more plainly and pointedly the dominant theme in John's proclamation (particularly in the earlier stage before the baptism of Jesus), namely, the impending judicial ordeal which would discriminate and separate between the chaff and the wheat, rendering a verdict of acceptance but also of rejection. The fact is that for such an interpretation of the rite there is ample biblical-historical justification.

[5] Malachi's own role as a messenger of the covenant lawsuit, already suggested by his name and manifest in the whole tenor of his message, is epitomized in his closing words (3:22-24 [4:4-6]) as he recalls the covenant transaction at Horeb and directs Israel's attention to the threatening eschatological curse.

[6] *Cf.*, *e.g.*, Ezek. 36:25; Zech. 13:1.

II. SYMBOLIC WATER ORDEAL

Appeal to the gods for judicial decision was a standard feature in ancient legal procedure. Varieties of trial by ordeal ranged all the way from the oath of the individual sworn under sanctions to be executed by the oath deities to international wars in settlement of covenant controversy, the disposition of the conflict being again the decision of the oath gods invoked in the treaties. The most graphic example of the ordeal technique in Israelite judicial practice was the jealousy ordeal prescribed in Numbers 5. A more familiar variety of ordeal was the drawing of lots to expose the guilty.[7] But apart from prescribed court procedure the principle of ordeal comes to expression in every judicial intervention of God in history.

The two common elemental forces that functioned as ordeal powers were water and fire. So it is, too, as Peter observes, in cosmic history. God's judgment of the ancient world was by water, and the day of judgment awaiting the present heaven and earth will be an ordeal by fire (II Pet. 3:5-7).

The water ordeal was long current in the ancient Near East. It was practiced throughout the Mesopotamian world and it is attested as early as the earliest known law code, that of the Sumerian Ur-Nammu.

Illustrative is the case dealt with in the second law of Hammurapi's Code. The accused was required to cast himself into the river. The word used for river in this law is preceded by the determinative for deity. The concept was, therefore, that the accused was casting himself into the hands of the divine judge who would declare the verdict. Emergence from the divine waters of ordeal would signify vindication: "If the River shows that man to be innocent and he comes forth safe," he shall dispossess his false accuser and the latter shall be put to death. But, "if the River overpowers him, his accuser shall take possession of his estate."[8]

Archetype of water ordeals was the Noahic deluge. The main features of the subsequent divine-river trials were all found in

[7] *E.g.*, Josh. 7:14; Jon. 1:7. According to one theory, the terms Urim and Thummim derive respectively from roots meaning "curse" and "be perfect." The objects so designated would then serve as ordeal devices, rendering one or the other verdict indicated by their names.

[8] That a similar river ordeal was practiced in the Ugarit area seems to be indicated by the use in Ugaritic mythology of the epithet "Judge River" for the god Yamm (Sea). *Cf.* C. H. Gordon, *Ugaritic Literature* (Rome, 1949), p. 11, n. 1.

the judgment of the flood: the direct revelation of divine verdict, the use of water as the ordeal element, the overpowering of the condemned and the deliverance of the justified, and the entrance of the ark-saved heirs of the new world into the possession of the erstwhile estates of the ungodly.

The other outstanding water ordeals of Old Testament history were those through which Moses and Joshua led Israel at the Red Sea and the Jordan. These, too, were acts of redemptive judgment wherein God vindicated the cause of those who called upon his name and condemned their adversaries. The exodus ordeal, with Israel coming forth safe and the Egyptians overwhelmed in the depths, strikingly exemplified the dual potential of the ordeal process. In the Jordan ordeal, the dispossession of the condemned by the acquitted was prominent. At that historical juncture the rightful ownership of Canaan was precisely the legal issue at stake, and God declared in favor of Israel by delivering them from Jordan's overflowing torrents. Thereby Israel's contemplated conquest of the land was vindicated as a holy war, a judgment of God. And the melting hearts of the Amorite and Canaanite kings, who grasped the legal significance of the episode as a divine verdict against them, were the inevitable psychological result (which would contribute in turn to the fulfillment of the verdict) in a culture where, even if superstitiously, the reality of the sacred ordeal was accepted.[9]

Since, then, the most memorable divine judgments of all covenant history had been trials by water ordeal and since John was sent to deliver the ultimatum of divine judgment, it does not appear too bold an interpretation of the baptismal sign of his mission to see in it a symbolic water ordeal, a dramatic enactment of the imminent messianic judgment. In such a visualization of the coming judgment John will have been resuming the prophetic tradition of picturing the messianic mission as a second Red Sea judgment (and so as a water ordeal).[10]

Indeed, read again in the light of the history of covenant ordeals, the whole record of John's ministry points to the understanding of his water rite as an ordeal sign rather than as a mere ceremonial bath of purification. The description of John's baptism as "unto the remission of sins," which is usually regarded as sug-

[9] See Josh. 5:1; *cf*. 2:10, 11; Ex. 15:13ff. The legal pattern of a trial by ordeal with its judicial cutting off and inheritance of land is pervasive in Ps. 37 (see esp. vv. 9ff., 22, 33f.).

[10] See, *e.g.*, Isa. 11:10-16 (cf. 27:1, 12, 13; 51:10, 11); Zech. 10:10, 11.

gesting the idea of spiritual cleansing, is even more compatible with the forensic conception of a verdict of acquittal rendered in a judicial ordeal. The time had come when here in the Jordan River, where once Yahweh had declared through an ordeal that the promised land belonged to Israel, he was requiring the Israelites to confess their forfeiture of the blessings of his kingdom and their liability to the wrath to come. Yet John's proclamation was a preaching of "good tidings" to the people (Lk. 3:18) because it invited the repentant to anticipate the messianic judgment in a symbolic ordeal in the Jordan, so securing for themselves beforehand a verdict of remission of sin against the coming judgment. To seal a holy remnant by baptism unto the messianic kingdom was the proper purpose of the bearer of the ultimatum of the Great King.

Further support for the interpretation of a baptismal rite as a sign of ordeal is found in the biblical use of $\beta\alpha\pi\tau\iota\zeta\omega$ (and $\beta\alpha\pi\tau\iota\sigma\mu\alpha$) to denote historic ordeals.[11] Paul described Israel's Red Sea ordeal as a being baptized (I Cor. 10:2) and Peter in effect calls the Noahic deluge ordeal a baptism (I Pet. 3:21). To these passages we shall want to return. But of particular relevance at this point is the fact that John the Baptist himself used the verb $\beta\alpha\pi\tau\iota\zeta\omega$ for the impending ordeal in which the One mightier than he would wield his winnowing fork to separate from the covenant kingdom those whose circumcision had by want of Abrahamic faith become uncircumcision and who must therefore be cut off from the congregation of Israel and devoted to unquenchable flames. With reference to this judicially discriminating ordeal with its dual destinies of garner and Gehenna John declared: "He shall baptize you with the Holy Ghost and with fire" (Matt. 3:11f.; Lk. 3:16f.; cf. Mk. 1:8). One of the Qumran hymns (1QH 3:28ff.) depicts an eschatological river of fire, "the torrents of Belial," and it has been suggested that possibly John had this in mind when he spoke of Jesus' baptizing with fire. Some would trace this image to Persian eschatology, which speaks of a river of molten metal through which all men must pass and in the ordeal process be either purified or destroyed.[12] For the back-

---

[11] Our concern here is not with the metaphorical use of $\beta\alpha\pi\tau\iota\zeta\omega$ in the sense of "overwhelm" (as in debts) but with the semantic development along the line of its technical religious usage.

[12] Cf. W. H. Brownlee, "John the Baptist in the New Light of Ancient Scrolls" in *The Scrolls and the New Testament*, ed. Krister Stendahl (New York, 1957), p. 42.

ground of John's thought, however, we must remember that fire was along with water a traditional ancient ordeal element. In fact, in the very prophecy where the Old Testament delineates the mission of the Lord and his Forerunner as final messengers of the covenant lawsuit, the messianic judgment is portrayed as an ordeal by fire with dual effects. For evildoers the fire of that day is the burning of an oven to consume them, but for those who fear God's name it is the healing rays of the sun to refine them (Mal. 3:19, 20 [4:1, 2]; *cf*. 3:2, 3).[13]

But John did more than describe the imminent messianic ordeal as an act of baptism. He instituted an explicit comparison between that baptismal ordeal which was to be executed by the coming One and his own baptismal rite: "I indeed baptize you with water . . . he shall baptize you with the Holy Ghost and with fire" (Matt. 3:11). John called attention to the great difference; his own baptism was only a symbol whereas the coming One would baptize men in an actual ordeal with the very elements of divine power. But the significant fact at present is not that John's baptism was only a symbol but that, according to his own exposition of it, what John's baptism symbolized was the coming messianic judgment. That is certainly the force of his double use of "baptize" in this comparison.

Jesus' reception of John's baptism can be more easily understood on this approach. As covenant Servant, Jesus submitted in symbol to the judgment of the God of the covenant in the waters of baptism. But for Jesus, as the Lamb of God, to submit to the symbol of judgment was to offer himself up to the curse of the covenant. By his baptism Jesus was consecrating himself unto his sacrificial death in the judicial ordeal of the cross.[14] Such an understanding of his baptism is reflected in Jesus' own reference

[13] In connection with the idea of a river of judgment fire, Daniel 7:9, 10 is of interest. From the throne of the Ancient of Days as he sits for judgment there issues a fiery stream. By it the horn making great kingdom claims is consumed (vv. 11, 26), while the kingdom taken from him is given to the vindicated saints of the Most High as an eternal possession (vv. 26, 27). The total structure of the passage thus follows the pattern of a judicial ordeal. Compare also the delivering-destroying heavenly fire and the lake of fire and brimstone in Rev. 20:9ff. See, too, our remarks on I Cor. 10:1ff. below.

[14] Agreeably, the heavenly verdict identifies Jesus as the Servant of Isaiah's songs (*cf*. Isa. 42:1), the one who must be led as a lamb to the slaughter and have laid upon him the iniquities of all his people. *Cf*. in this connection the comments of Cullmann (*Baptism in the New Testament* [Chicago, 1950], pp. 20f.) on the Baptist's testimony in John 1:29-34.

to his coming passion as a baptism: "I have a baptism to be baptized with" (Lk. 12:50; *cf.* Mk. 10:38).[15] Jesus' symbolic baptism unto judgment appropriately concluded with a divine verdict, the verdict of justification expressed by the heavenly voice and sealed by the Spirit's anointing, Messiah's earnest of the kingdom inheritance (Matt. 3:16, 17; Mk. 1:10, 11; Lk. 3:22; *cf.* Jn. 1:32, 33; Ps. 2:7f.). This verdict of sonship was contested by Satan, and that led to the ordeal by combat between Jesus and Satan, beginning with the wilderness temptation immediately after Jesus' baptism and culminating in the crucifixion and resurrection-vindication of the victorious Christ, the prelude to his reception of all the kingdoms of the world (the issue under dispute in the ordeal; *cf.* esp. Matt. 4:8ff.; Lk. 4:5ff.).[16]

Further background for Jesus' conceptualizing of his sufferings as a water ordeal (and at the same time an additional antecedent for John's introduction of a water rite symbolic of judicial ordeal) is found in those supplicatory Psalms in which the righteous servant pleads for deliverance from overwhelming waters. Of particular interest is Psalm 69, from which the New Testament draws so deeply in its explication of the judicial sufferings of Christ: "I am come into deep waters, where the floods overflow me. . . . Let not the waterflood overflow me, neither let the deep swallow me up" (vv. 2b, 15a; *cf.* vv. 1, 2a, 14).[17] The currency of this imagery in the days of John and Jesus is attested by the Qumran hymns.[18] The ultimate judicial origin of the figure in the literal practice of trial by water is evidenced by the judicial atmosphere and structuring of Psalms in which it appears. The suppliant pleads in the language of the law court. Against the lying accusations of his adversaries he protests his innocence and appeals for a manifestation of divine justice, that is, for deliverance out of his ordeal.[19] The suppliant Jonah found it possible to make

---

[15] In the context of that statement Jesus seems to allude in other ways, too, to the Forerunner's witness to him. He says that his mission is one of casting fire on the earth (Lk. 12:49; *cf.* Matt. 3:11; Lk. 3:16) and that it will result in a division among men (Lk. 12:51ff.; *cf.* Matt. 3:12; Lk. 3:17).

[16] See further the discussion of Col. 2:11ff. below. *Cf.* Rom. 1:4.

[17] See also Pss. 18:16, 17 (15, 16); 42:8 (7); *cf.* 68:23 (22); 124:4, 5; 144:7.

[18] See, *e.g.*, 1QH 3:19ff.; 5 (pervasively); 6:22ff., *cf.* 32ff.

[19] Note, for example, Pss. 18:7 (6) (*cf.* I Kings 8:31f.), 21-25 (20-24); 43:1 (viewed as part of a single complex comprising Pss. 42 and

literal use of this terminology of water ordeal in his appeal from the depths, and Jesus saw in Jonah's trial by water the sign of his own judgment ordeal in the heart of the earth (Jon. 2:2ff. [1ff.]; Matt. 12:39, 40).

Synonymous with the motif of the ordeal by water is that of ordeal by combat with sea-monsters. Thus, the Red Sea water ordeal becomes in certain Old Testament passages a conflict of Yahweh against Leviathan (Isa. 51:9, 10; *cf.* Pss. 74:12-15; 89:10, 11 [9, 10]). We are thereby reminded that the Lord was present with his people in the passage through the sea, that he underwent their ordeal, and that their salvation depended on their identification with him. Then in the New Testament there is a typological application of this imagery to Jesus' conflict with Satan in the course of his humiliation unto death.[20] Hence, on our understanding of John's baptism in general and of his baptism of Jesus in particular, Jesus' experience in the Jordan would have been a symbolic anticipation of his ensuing victorious combat with the Satan-Dragon. We cannot, therefore, but view with new appreciation the liturgies of the ancient church when they speak of Jesus crushing the head of the dragon in his descent into the river for baptism.[21]

It was with valid insight that early baptismal prayers recited the Lord's supernatural way in the waters in events like creation, the deluge, and the Red Sea and Jordan crossings. Singularly apposite is the anchoring of God's redemptive acts of subduing and dividing the ordeal waves in his creation acts of dividing and bounding the chaos waters in order that the dry land, inheritance of man, might appear. (It may be recalled here that in ancient mythology the slaying of the chaos dragon is the necessary preliminary to the establishment of the world order.) There is indeed an allegorical strain in these ancient prayers, but they did achieve a live sense of identification with the eschatological cur-

---

43); 69 (throughout, considered particularly in its messianic realization). Of interest here are the form-critical views of H. Schmidt concerning the so-called individual laments and especially the identity of the enemies of the Psalmist.

[20] See especially Revelation 12, which symbolizes the Satanic enmity as both dragon and flood. Note the points of contact between this vision and 1QH 5. *Cf.* the observations on the baptism of Jesus above.

[21] *Cf.* Per Lundberg, *La typologie baptismale dans l'ancienne Église* (Leipzig and Uppsala, 1942), pp. 10ff., 225ff., 229ff.

rent of redemptive history, something our denatured modern baptismal liturgies would do well to recapture.

Conclusions: John the Baptist was sent as a messenger of the Old Covenant to its final generation. His concern was not to prepare the world at large for the coming of Christ but to summon Israel unto the Lord to whom they had sworn allegiance at Sinai, ere his wrath broke upon them and the Mosaic kingdom was terminated in the flames of messianic judgment. The demand which John brought to Israel was focused in his call to baptism. This baptism was not an ordinance to be observed by Israel in their generations but a special sign for that terminal generation epitomizing the particular crisis in covenant history represented by the mission of John as messenger of the Lord's ultimatum.

From the angle of repentance and faith, John's ultimatum could be seen as a gracious invitation to the marriage feast of the Suzerain's Son; and John's baptism, as a seal of the remission of sins. Bright with promise in this regard was Jesus' submission to John's baptism. For the passing of Jesus through the divine judgment in the water rite in the Jordan meant to John's baptism what the passing of Yahweh through the curse of the knife rite of Genesis 15 meant to Abraham's circumcision. In each case the divine action constituted an invitation to all recipients of these covenant signs of consecration to identify themselves by faith with the Lord himself in their passage through the ordeal. So they might be assured of emerging from the overwhelming curse with a blessing. Jesus' passage through the water ordeal with the others who were baptized in the Jordan was also one in meaning with the Lord's presence with Israel in the theophany pillar during the passage through the Red Sea, and in the ark of the covenant during their crossing of the Jordan.[22] And the meaning of all these acts of the Lord of the covenant is expressed in the promise: "But now thus saith the Lord that created thee, O Jacob, and he that formed thee, O Israel, Fear not: for I have redeemed thee, I have called thee by thy name; thou art mine. When thou passest through the waters, I will be with thee; and through the rivers, they shall not overflow thee: when thou walkest through the fire, thou shalt not be burned; neither shall the flame kindle upon thee. For I am the Lord thy God, the Holy One of Israel, thy Saviour" (Isa. 43:1-3a).

---

[22] Notice the cursing of the curse in these episodes where the ordeal waters themselves become the objects of the circumcision curse of division and cutting off.

Viewed from a more comprehensive vantage point, John's baptism was a sign of the ordeal through which Israel must pass to receive a judgment of either curse or blessing, for it represented the demand of a suzerainty-law covenant, an engagement sealed by dual sanctions.[23] The actual judgment, experienced by that generation to which John was sent, was an ordeal unto the cursing and casting off of Israel, a remnant only being excepted (*cf.* Rom. 11). The city and the sanctuary were destroyed and the end thereof was with a flood, a pouring out of desolation (*cf.* Dan. 9:26, 27). To this overflowing wrath the waters of John's baptism had pointed, as well as to the remission of sins received by the remnant according to the election of grace.

By his message and baptism John thus proclaimed again to the seed of Abraham the meaning of their circumcision. Circumcision was no guarantee of inviolable privilege. It was a sign of the divine ordeal in which the axe, laid unto the roots of the unfruitful trees cursed by Messiah, would cut them off (Matt. 3:10; Lk. 3:9). John's baptism was in effect a recircumcising.[24]

---

[23] See above, Chapter Two, under "The Priority of Law."

[24] As observed above, the Noahic deluge was archetypal among the ancient water judgments from which New Testament baptismal rites drew their ordeal significance. It is more than interesting, then, that in Gen. 9:11 the flood is viewed as the cutting-off curse of the covenant: "I establish my covenant with you, that never again shall all flesh be cut off by the waters of a flood" (*RSV*). The same play on פָּרַת, "cut (off)," (*cf.* "cut a covenant") is used with reference to the flood waters here as is found with circumcision in Gen. 17:14. (Note, too, the coincidental use of בָּשָׂר, "flesh," in both passages.) From a biblical viewpoint, therefore, circumcision and baptism are related to a common symbolic source; for the waters of the flood were a proto-circumcision as well as a proto-baptism.

CHAPTER FIVE

CHRISTIAN BAPTISM: OATH-SIGN OF THE NEW COVENANT

One of the links between Christian and Johannine baptism is the baptism which Jesus authorized and his disciples administered during the very period of John's preaching and baptizing (John 3:22; 4:1f.). The key to the meaning of that early dominical baptism and to the enigma of its apparently abrupt cessation is to be found in the significance of the role of John and of Jesus as messengers of the covenant lawsuit.[1]

When Jesus began his public ministry, God's lawsuit with Israel was in the ultimatum stage. At this point, the judicial function of Jesus coincided with that of John. Jesus' witness had the effect of confirming John's witness of final warning to Israel, especially to Israel's officialdom in the Judean area. And since the meaning of the baptismal rite administered by these messengers of the covenant derived from the official nature of their mission, the import of Jesus' baptism, though separately conducted, would also be essentially the same as John's. Thus, as a sign of the covenant lawsuit against Israel, the baptismal rite of Jesus was, like John's, a symbol of the imminent judgment ordeal of the people of the Old Covenant.

This interpretation of Jesus' early baptizing in terms of the concurrent ultimatum mission of John is strikingly confirmed by the evident cessation of that baptism once John was imprisoned.

---

[1] *Cf.* above, Chapter Four, under "Messenger of Ultimatum." See G. R. Beasley-Murray, *Baptism in the New Testament* (London, 1963), pp. 67ff., for a survey of treatments of these questions. He comments: "If Jesus did refrain from letting His disciples baptize in the later ministry, we have to admit that the reason is shrouded in uncertainty" (p. 70).

By suffering the voice in the wilderness to be silenced, the Lord of the covenant concluded the ultimatum stage in his lawsuit against Israel, judging that Israel's responsible representatives had by now decisively rejected his warning. The profound satisfaction which the defiant rulers must have registered at John's imprisonment was, it would seem, the final, intolerable expression of their contempt for the heavenly authority in which John had come to them (*cf.* Matt. 21:23ff.; Mk. 11:22ff.; Lk. 20:1ff.). Hence, the imprisonment of John was the signal for the departure of Jesus to Galilee. The form of presentation in the Gospels, particularly in Matthew and Mark, is such as to call attention to the fact that it was the imprisonment of John that prompted Jesus to initiate the new ministry in Galilee, whose epochal nature the Synoptics are clearly concerned to impress on us (Matt. 4:12ff.; Mk. 1:14f.; *cf.* Lk. 4:14; Jn. 4:1-3; Acts 10:37). The Synoptics begin here to record the teaching of Jesus with its announcement that now the time was fulfilled and the kingdom at hand (Matt. 4:17; Mk. 1:15), and with its heralding, in the Nazareth synagogue, of the arrival of the acceptable year of the Lord (Lk. 4:19, 21). Thus, implicitly, the Gospels trace to John's imprisonment the ending of the early Judean ministry of Jesus with its particular baptismal rite. That is, they implicitly connect the cessation of Jesus' early baptism with the termination of the ultimatum stage in the covenant lawsuit against Israel.[2]

In brief, then, the early baptism authorized by Jesus was a sign of God's ultimatum to Israel. When that ultimatum was emphatically rejected, a new phase in the administration of the covenant was entered, Jesus' ministry of baptism ceasing along with the Johannine message of ultimatum which it had sealed.

The difference between the earlier and the later baptisms authorized by Jesus was the difference between two quite distinct periods in the history of the covenant. The later baptism was of course ordained as a sign of the New Covenant; it was not part of the old lawsuit against Israel. Nevertheless, this new water baptism, appearing so soon after the other and still within the

---

[2] John's Gospel indicates that the concluding of the Judean ministry and the new beginning in Galilee were attributable to a hostile reaction of the Pharisees to Jesus himself (4:1). The response to the ultimatum of the two messengers of the covenant would naturally be similar. His royal summons spurned by Israel's hierarchical powers, Jesus turned to the task of calling the remnant out of the shepherdless flock and thereby saving them from the now certain judgment (*cf.* Zech. 11).

personal ministry of Jesus, would hardly bear a meaning altogether different from the earlier one. There would be a pronounced continuity between Christian baptism and the earlier, Johannine baptism. While, therefore, the baptismal ordinance which Christ appointed to his church would have a significance appropriate to the now universal character of the covenant community and to its new eschatological metaphysic, it would continue to be a sign of consecration to the Lord of the covenant and, more particularly, a symbolic passage through the judicial ordeal, in which those under the rule of the covenant receive a definitive verdict for eternal glory or for perpetual desolation. This is borne out by the New Testament evidence.

I. BAPTISM AS ORDEAL

That Peter conceived of Christian baptism as a sign of judicial ordeal is indicated by his likening it to the archetypal water ordeal, the Noahic deluge (I Pet. 3:20-22). In this passage, $\dot{\alpha}\nu\tau\acute{\iota}\tau\nu\pi o\nu$ (v. 21) is best taken with $\beta\acute{\alpha}\pi\tau\iota\sigma\mu\alpha$, in which case Christian baptism is directly designated as the antitype of the ordeal waters of the deluge, or of the passage through those waters.[3] But even if $\dot{\alpha}\nu\tau\acute{\iota}\tau\nu\pi o\nu$ were connected with $\dot{\upsilon}\mu\hat{\alpha}s$ so that the church would be called the antitype of the Noahic family, the total comparison drawn by Peter would still involve an interpretation of the baptismal waters in terms of the significance of the deluge ordeal.

With respect to the interpretation of the deluge-"baptism" as a judicial ordeal, we would observe that that understanding of it opens the way for a satisfactory carrying through of what would seem the most straightforward approach to these difficult verses. For the most natural assumption is certainly that Peter was led to bring the deluge and the rite of baptism together because of the common element of the waters. And surely, then, that exegesis will most commend itself which succeeds in maintaining a genuine parallel between the role played by the waters in the two cases. Since, therefore, a saving function is predicated of the

[3] It is a question of whether the relative pronoun ὅ at the beginning of verse 21 refers to the immediately preceding δι' ὕδατος (understood instrumentally) or to the more general idea of verse 20 (the δι' ὕδατος then being understood locally). The acceptance of the textual variant ᾧ would not affect this choice; it would make it possible to take the Νῶε of verse 20 as the antecedent.

waters of baptism (v. 21), the waters should also figure as a means of salvation in the deluge episode (v. 20). That is, the problematic δι' ὕδατος should be construed in the instrumental sense. This can be done, and without the tortuous explanations required by the usual forms of this approach, once it is recognized that the flood waters were the ordeal instrument by which God justified Noah.[4] It may be natural to think of the flood waters as merely destructive, as something from which to be saved. But those waters may in precisely the same and obvious sense be the means of condemnation-destruction or of justification-salvation, if they are seen to be the waters of a judicial ordeal with its potential of dual divine verdicts.

According to another suggestion,[5] Peter meant that the flood waters saved Noah by delivering him from the evil of man (*cf.* II Pet. 2:5, 7). A similar aspect of Christian baptism is then found in Peter's baptismal call to the Israelites on Pentecost to save themselves from their crooked generation (Acts 2:40f.). It might also be observed that the extrication of the righteous from their persecution by the ungodly is characteristic of redemptive judgments and that the oppressive violence practiced by the pre-diluvian kings figures prominently in the introduction to the flood record.[6] Nevertheless, a forensic interpretation of the salvation referred to in I Peter 3:20 is preferable since the judicial relationship of God to man is a more prominent aspect of both biblical soteriology and the symbolism of baptism.[7] Moreover, Peter proceeds immediately to develop the idea of salvation, as signified in baptism, the counterpart to the flood, in specifically forensic terms (see vv. 21b, 22).

That which signalized salvation was not, says Peter, the mere putting away of the filth of the flesh incidental to a water rite. It was rather the good conscience of the baptized (v. 21b). Now conscience has to do with accusing and excusing; it is forensic.

---

[4] The author of Hebrews also interpreted the deluge in the terms of the ordeal paradigm: righteousness, condemnation, inheritance (see Heb. 11:7).

[5] See Bo Reicke, *The Anchor Bible: The Epistles of James, Peter, and Jude* (New York, 1964), p. 113.

[6] *Cf.* Gen. 6:2, 4f., 13. See my "Divine Kingship and Genesis 6:1-4" in *The Westminster Theological Journal*, 24, 2 (May, 1962), 191ff.

[7] Also, Acts 2:40f. is better understood as a call to escape from that crooked generation regarded as the target of threatening divine wrath. Note the similarities to the terminology and message of John the Baptist (*cf.* Lk. 3:5ff.).

Baptism, then, is concerned with man in the presence of God's judgment throne. This conclusion remains undisturbed whatever the precise exegesis of the relevant phrase. The ἐπερώτημα seems best understood as a pledge (a meaning well attested in judicial texts), the solemn vow of consecration given in answer to the introductory questions put to the candidate for baptism. In ancient covenant procedure, as has been observed above, such an oath of allegiance was accompanied by rites symbolizing the ordeal sanctions of the covenant. If ἐπερώτημα were taken as an appeal, either the appeal of a good conscience to God or the appeal to God for a good conscience, it would refer to the prayer uttered in prospect of the divine ordeal.[8] There is a further heightening of the juridical emphasis in this passage in Peter's reference to the actual saving act with respect to which baptism serves as a symbolic means of grace (vv. 21c, 22). The salvation figured forth in baptism is that accomplished in the judgment of Christ, which issued in his resurrection. The motif of ordeal by combat is introduced by the allusion to Christ's subjugation of angels, authorities, and powers.[9] Thus the total context of Peter's thought concerning baptism supports the conclusion we have drawn from his comparison of baptism to the deluge, namely, that he conceived of this sacrament as a sign of judicial ordeal.

Paul saw the nature of baptism displayed in another classic Old Testament water ordeal. In I Corinthians 10:1ff. the apostle recalls that the Mosaic generation of Israel participated in events that corresponded in religious significance to the church's sacramental ordinances of baptism and the Lord's Supper.[10] Yet, in

---

[8] *Cf.* further E. G. Selwyn, *The First Epistle of Peter* (London, 1946), pp. 205f.; Bo Reicke, *op. cit.*, pp. 114f. and *The Disobedient Spirits and Christian Baptism* (Copenhagen, 1946), pp. 182ff. Reicke maintains that in this epistle συνείδησις does not mean "conscience" but "consent" or "positive attitude." In 3:21 he translates: "a pledge of good will to God," that is, a promise of loyalty. By placing baptism in the context of an oath of allegiance this exegesis, too, is favorable to the interpretation of baptism as an ordeal ritual.

[9] *Cf.* below on Col. 2:11f. On the early church's association of baptism with the deluge and of both with the overcoming of the demonic powers of the abyss, see Lundberg, *La typologie baptismale dans l'ancienne Église*, pp. 73ff.

[10] H. H. Rowley remarks that Paul "is really concerned to stress the contrast between that crossing [*i.e.*, through the Red Sea] and baptism" (*The Unity of the Bible* [Philadelphia, 1953], p. 149, n. 1). But the force of Paul's warning depends precisely on the similarity of privilege enjoyed

spite of experiencing the sacramental privileges of the Mosaic Covenant, most of that generation fell beneath its curses because of defection from their sworn allegiance to Yahweh. Therein was a message for the church which Paul proceeded to apply. Our present interest, however, is in verse 2: "(they) were all baptized into Moses in the cloud and in the sea."

As was observed previously, the passage through the Red Sea had the character of a judicial ordeal by which Israel was vindicated and Egypt doomed. It was an ordeal by water and by fire, the two elemental ordeal powers. The water needs no further explanation; perhaps the fire does.[11]

In his theophanic embodiment in the pillar of smoke and fire, Yahweh, himself a consuming fire, was present in judgment.[12] Through the fiery judgment pillar he could declare and execute his verdicts unto salvation or damnation. The fire-theophany at the burning but unconsumed bush was a token of Israel's safe passage through the imminent ordeal. In the exodus crisis the pillar served to shelter, guide, and protect the elect nation; it thereby rendered for Israel a favorable verdict (*cf.* Ex. 13:21f.; 14:19f.). But through the pillar a judgment of condemnation was declared against the Egyptians as the Lord, looking forth from the fire-cloud, discomfited them (*cf.* Ex. 14:20, 24ff.).[13]

The presence of the cloud-pillar theophany (see Ex. 19:18 [*cf.* Heb. 12:18-29]; 24:16f.; 33:19; Num. 12:10; 14:10ff.; 16:19, 42; 20:6), at times clearly functioning as Yahweh's ordeal by fire, is mentioned in various other judicial situations in the Mosaic history. In an eschatological context, Isaiah associates the theophany pillar with a discriminatory, purgative burning process which leaves in Zion a holy remnant for whom the fiery pillar is a defense and glory (Isa. 4:2-5). In Revelation 15, the imagery

---

in the exodus crossing and in Christian baptism, the contrast being between Israel's post-"baptismal" behavior and the post-baptismal conduct to which Paul exhorts Christians.

[11] *Cf.* above, pp. 55, 57f.

[12] The Apocalyptist beheld the exalted Christ as a veritable incarnation of this theophanic glory pillar, appropriately present for judgment (Rev. 1:13ff.). The ordeal elements of the waters and sword are included in the picture as subordinate details (vv. 15f.).

[13] According to E. A. Speiser's rendering of Ex. 14:20, the pillar of cloud is said to curse, or cast a spell upon, the night. See his "An Angelic 'Curse': Exodus 14:20" in the *Journal of the American Oriental Society*, 80, 3 (July-Sept., 1960), 198-200.

of which seems to draw upon the Red Sea triumph (*cf.* especially vv. 2f.), the elements of the sea and fire (v. 2) and the flashing glory of the theophanic smoke-cloud (v. 8) are combined to introduce the mission of the seven angels who pour out the vials of ultimate divine wrath (v. 1; *cf.* chapter 16). The earth is thereby brought into its final ordeal, which has a dual issue in the destruction of the harlot city, Babylon, and the exaltation of the bride city, Jerusalem. The latter, according to the regular pattern of the law of ordeal, enters into possession of the disputed inheritance. Each of these judicial outcomes is appropriately introduced by one of these angels of the final ordeal (17:1 and 21:9). This reflects the teaching of Jesus, where angels function as God's ordeal power, the ordeal knife that severs the wicked unto the furnace of fire (Matt. 13:49; 21:31; Mk. 13:27).[14] For the earliest revelation of the role of angels as instruments of judgment by fire and sword see Genesis 3:24.[15]

The exodus judgment was then an ordeal by fire-cloud and water, and it was this ordeal that Paul identified as a baptism. If there were any doubt that "baptized" in I Corinthians 10:2 is to be taken not as a common verb but in its technical religious sense, it would be dispelled by the addition of "into Moses," which unmistakably carries through the parallel to the Pauline phrase, "baptized into Jesus Christ."[16] Besides, none of the non-technical meanings of $\beta\alpha\pi\tau\acute{\iota}\zeta\omega$ (*e.g.*, dip, immerse, plunge, sink, drench, overwhelm) would accurately describe the physical relationship that actually obtained between Israel and the fire and water. In fact, neither baptismal element so much as came in contact with an Israelite during the crossing. Moreover, if in its technical employment as a water rite $\beta\alpha\pi\tau\acute{\iota}\zeta\omega$ denoted a washing or cleans-

[14] *Cf.* Louis A. Vos, *The Synoptic Traditions in the Apocalypse* (Kampen, 1965), pp. 148ff.

[15] In view of the association of the Red Sea with baptism in I Cor. 10:2, E. Käsemann asks whether the heavenly sea of Rev. 15:2 ought not to be connected with the waters of baptism ("A Primitive Christian Baptismal Liturgy" in *Essays on New Testament Themes* [Naperville, 1964], p. 161). This viewpoint is more positively presented by A. Farrer, *The Revelation of St. John the Divine* (Oxford, 1964), pp. 90f., 171f. *Cf.* Lundberg, *op. cit.*, p. 143.

[16] Lundberg (*op. cit.*, pp. 140-142) would support this conclusion on the ground that the baptism "in the cloud" is cited as an equivalent to being baptized "by one Spirit" (I Cor. 12:13). He notes Mk. 9:7; Lk. 1:35; and the use of $\dot{\epsilon}\pi\iota\sigma\kappa\iota\acute{\alpha}\zeta\epsilon\iota\nu$ in the *LXX* for the descent of the cloud. *Cf.* Matt. 3:11.

ing, we could not account for Paul's usage in I Corinthians 10:2. For the effect of the passage through the Red Sea was not a cleansing of the Israelites—may they not even have been a little dustier when they reached the far shore? Also, the idea of washing would not readily account for the "into Moses" aspect of this baptism.[17] If, on the other hand, we grant that technical, ritual baptism signified for Paul a process of judicial ordeal, his placing of the Red Sea crossing in the category of baptism makes transparent sense. What the apostle meant when he said that the fathers were baptized into Moses in their passage under the cloud and through the sea was that the Lord thereby brought them into an ordeal by those elements, an ordeal through which he declared them accepted as the servant people of his covenant and so under the authority of Moses, his mediatorial vicegerent.[18]

We would judge, therefore, that for Paul, as for Peter, the sacrament of Christian baptism signified a trial by ordeal and that the term $\beta\alpha\pi\tau\acute{\iota}\zeta\omega$, in its secondary, technical usage, had reference to the ordeal character of a person's encounter with the baptismal element.

Thoroughly congenial to the ordeal interpretation of the baptismal symbolism is the New Testament's exposition of baptism as a participation with Christ in the judgment ordeal of his death, burial, and resurrection (see Rom. 6:3ff.; Col. 2:11ff.; *cf.* I Cor. 1:13; Lk. 12:50). We shall concentrate here on Colossians 2:11ff.

[17] On the assumption that the place of Israel's crossing, *yam sûph*, means "sea of reeds," it has been suggested that this name may have brought to the mind of the author of Exodus the Sea of Reeds which figures in Egyptian mythology. This sea (also known as a sea of the underworld and of heaven and of life) was a sea of purification through which the soul must pass for regeneration. (So J. R. Towers, "The Red Sea" in *Journal of Near Eastern Studies*, 18 [1959], 150-153.) But the explanation of Paul's use of $\beta\alpha\pi\tau\acute{\iota}\zeta\omega$ must be sought elsewhere. On the meaning of the Hebrew *yam sûph*, *cf.* M. Copisarow, "The Ancient Egyptian, Greek and Hebrew Concept of the Red Sea," in *Vetus Testamentum*, 12 (1962), 1-13.

[18] *Cf.* my *TGK*, pp. 30, 36f.; *cf.* R. Schnackenburg, *Baptism in the Thought of St. Paul* (New York, 1964) (tr. G. R. Beasley-Murray), p. 23. That baptism, for Paul, was an act that conveyed one through death into the new world is maintained by Lundberg (*op. cit.*, pp. 135ff.) on the ground that there was current a similar interpretation of the Red Sea episode, to which Paul likened Christian baptism. He also assembles the evidence for the early prevalence of the conception of baptism as a passage through the waters of death. It would appear that the thesis of the present chapter, though not identical with that conception, is compatible with it and in any case restores baptism to the general world of ideas with which it was associated in at least some ancient liturgies.

because in this passage there is a noteworthy interrelating of biblical ordeal symbols and realities in explication of Christ's sufferings and triumph.

Earlier we followed the exegesis of "the circumcision of Christ" (Col. 2:11) that regards "of Christ" as an objective genitive and "the circumcision," therefore, as the crucifixion of Christ. "Without hands" would then mean that his circumcision was no mere human symbolization of the curse sanction of the law but the actual divine judgment. "Putting off the body of flesh" would further contrast the crucifixion to the symbolic removal of the foreskin as being a perfecting of circumcision in a complete cutting off unto death, and that as an object of divine cursing. This would accord with Paul's usage in Colossians 1:22 (*cf.* Eph. 2:15f.). According to another interpretation of the verse, "of Christ" is a subjective genitive and "the circumcision" is a spiritual circumcision experienced by the one who is in Christ, namely, crucifixion of the old man, or destruction of the body of sin. "Putting off the body of flesh" is thus understood according to the thought of Colossians 3:9 (*cf.*, *e.g.*, Rom. 6:6 with its similar context). This circumcision would be "without hands" as a divinely wrought spiritual reality, not a mere external symbol.

The choice between these two interpretations is difficult.[19] But even if this "circumcision of Christ" is understood as an experience of the Christian, it is still one which he has in his identification with Christ in his crucifixion. For in this passage as a whole (including now verses 11a and 12), Christian experience is modelled by Paul after the pattern of Christ's death, burial, and resurrection, the Christian's circumcision (v. 11a) corresponding to Christ's death. As noted earlier, where the same pattern emerges in Romans 6:3ff., the first step is called death, whereas in Colossians 2:11 it is circumcision. If, then, Paul calls the Christian death-experience a circumcision it is only because he was first of all prepared to call Christ's death a circumcision. Our conception of the crucifixion ordeal is thereby enriched with the thought associations of the ancient sign of the ritual knife ordeal. So, for example, the crucifixion is linked to the Genesis 15 circumcision-oath of the Lord as fulfillment to symbolic prophecy. Incidentally, since the theophany in Genesis 15 is essentially the ordeal fire-cloud, the remarkable picture presented there is that of the divine

---

[19] F. F. Bruce combines them in his exegesis (E. K. Simpson and F. F. Bruce, *Commentary on the Epistles to the Ephesians and the Colossians* [Grand Rapids, 1957], p. 235).

fire ordeal itself undergoing division in the covenantal knife ordeal.

Paul's delineation of the death of Christ includes the additional ordeal feature of decision rendered through combat (v. 15). A legal setting is already indicated in verse 14 by the statement that the curse claim of the law was satisfied on the cross. Possibly the figure of the χειρόγραφον and its "blotting out" (ἐξαλείψας) was suggested to Paul by the jealousy ordeal of Numbers 5, which prescribed a handwritten document and a "blotting out" (the same verb in the *LXX*). The χειρόγραφον would then contain the curses of the covenant sworn to by its members and blotted out by being visited on Christ on the cross, just as the curses of the jealousy document sworn to by the woman in her oath of clearance were obliterated only in an act of divine judgment, being absorbed into the water drunk by the woman and so made the instrument of the ordeal verdict. A further legal element in the Colossians 2 context is the accusing role of Satan in the judgment of God's people, which is suggested by the demonic antagonists who face Christ in his judgment conflict (v. 15).[20] It is by victory in this combat with Satan's hosts that the vindication of Christ and the acquittal of those who are united with him in his ordeal are secured. Again in the New Testament Apocalypse the verdict against the Accuser is declared through a battle ordeal (Rev. 12:7ff.). Christ's triumphing involves an action denoted by the problematic ἀπεκδυσάμενος (Col. 2:15). According to a popular exegesis of this term, Christ stripped the vanquished principalities and powers of their armor. In that case we might compare the imagery to the ordeal combat of the champions David and Goliath, wherein, Yahweh having judged in favor of Israel, David stripped the giant of his armor and carried it away in triumph (*cf.* I Sam. 17:54). But it is worth considering whether the figurative allusion in Colossians 2:15 is not rather to the well-

---

[20] In Jewish apocalyptic, χειρόγραφον is found as the designation of a book held by an accusing angel and recording sins which the seer desires blotted out. See the discussion of A. J. Bandstra, *The Law and the Elements of the World* (Kampen, 1964), pp. 164ff. Bandstra's own view of the passage as a whole is distinctive. Following O. A. Blanchette, he takes χειρόγραφον as a metaphor for our sinful flesh as borne by Christ and regards that, rather than the principalities and powers or some object understood (so the Latin fathers), as the object of ἀπεκδυσάμενος.

attested ancient practice of belt-wrestling as a combat-ordeal technique in court procedure. Victory and favorable verdict were achieved by stripping off the adversary's wrestling belt.[21] It is perhaps significant that the principalities and powers of Colossians 2:15 appear in the closely related Pauline letter to the Ephesians as the opponents of Christians in their "wrestling" (Eph. 6:12). According to this interpretation of ἀπεκδυσάμενος (and relating it to the ἀπέκδυσις of verse 11), the passage would mean that Christ in his very suffering of the circumcision-curse of crucifixion accomplished the circumcision-stripping off of his demonic opponents. The divine verdict was registered in the triumphant emergence of Christ from the domain of death; our Lord "was raised again for our justification" (Rom. 4:25b). His death-burial-resurrection was then a victory over the accusers, a stripping away of their legal claims, exposing, overcoming, and casting them out through the belt-grappling of a divine ordeal.

Graphic confirmation of the ordeal significance of baptism is thus found in the Pauline integration of baptism with the messianic death-burial-resurrection schema, especially where Paul expounds the latter as both a circumcision and a judicial ordeal by combat.

Mention must be made of the common significance of baptism and circumcision which emerges so clearly in this same connection. Paul understood both of these rituals as signs made with hands, signifying union with Christ in his representative judgment ordeal. He also interpreted both as signs of the corresponding spiritual death and resurrection of believers. Especially remarkable is the ease with which Paul in Colossians 2:11f. combines circumcision with baptism as complementary signs of the death-burial-resurrection pattern, whereas elsewhere (Rom. 6:3ff.) baptism by itself serves as a sign of the entire complex.

II. NEW COVENANT JUDGMENT

Is the interpretation of Christian baptism as a sign of covenantal judgment ordeal compatible with the biblical teaching con-

[21] See C. H. Gordon, "Belt-wrestling in the Bible World," *Hebrew Union College Annual*, Part One, 1950-1951, pp. 131-136. *Cf.* my commentary on Job in *The Wycliffe Bible Commentary*, ed. C. F. Pfeiffer and E. F. Harrison (Chicago, 1962), pp. 486-488. In Col. 2:15, ἀπεκδυσάμενος would be an indirect middle.

cerning the newness of the New Covenant? Even if the earlier covenants were law covenants enforceable by dual sanctions, with both the blessing and the curse signified by the sign of circumcision, the question may still be raised whether the introduction of the new order did not constitute so radical a change as to transform the covenant into an administration exclusively of blessing. Is not that the force, for example, of Jeremiah's prophecy of the New Covenant? And must not the baptismal sign of the New Covenant differ, then, in this respect from the old consecration sign of circumcision?

This problem was anticipated in the development of our biblico-theological definition of covenant.[22] Law was there shown to be a fundamental element in the Covenant of Redemption. With respect to the redemptive revelation at last given in Christ, the revelation which *is* the New Covenant, it was observed that for Christ, as the covenant Servant and second Adam, the redemptive mission was comprehensively one of obedience to the law of the covenant as the way to secure the covenant's blessings. The proper purpose of the New Covenant was found to be realized precisely in this, that Christ through his active and passive obedience as the representative of his people and for their salvation honored the law of the kingdom of God in its abiding stipulations and sanctions even as revealed from the beginning in the Covenant of Creation and as republished in the redemptive administrations of the Old Testament. Whatever it is, therefore, that constitutes the newness of the New Covenant, it is not the negation of its law character, law being understood as the principle that makes kingdom inheritance dependent on the obedience of a representative federal head. Indeed, this aspect of the essential law character of the Covenant of Redemption is nowhere more clearly displayed than here in the New Covenant, its perfecting administration.

Moreover, the newness of the New Covenant does not consist in a reduction of the Covenant of Redemption to the principle of election and guaranteed blessing. Its law character is seen in this, too, that it continues to be a covenant with dual sanctions. In this connection, account must be taken of Jeremiah's classic prophecy of the New Covenant (Jer. 31:31ff.). Since exegesis has often erred by way of an oversimplified stress on the difference or new-

---

[22] See Chapter Two above.

ness of the divine work promised in this passage,[23] it is important to mark the continuity that is evident even here between the New and the Old Covenants. For all its difference, the New Covenant of Jeremiah 31 is still patterned after the Sinaitic Covenant. In fact, Jeremiah's concept of the New Covenant was a development of that already presented by Moses in the sanctions section of the Deuteronomic renewal of the Sinaitic Covenant (Deut. 30:1-10). According to Jeremiah, the New Covenant is a writing of the law on the heart rather than on tables of stone (v. 33; cf. II Cor. 3:3), but it is another writing of the law. [24] It is a new law covenant.[25] Hence, for Jeremiah, the New Covenant, though it could be sharply contrasted with the Old (v. 32), was nevertheless a renewal of the Mosaic Covenant. It belonged to the familiar administrative pattern of periodic covenant renewal (of which the cycle of sabbatical years was an expression), and renewal is the exponent of continuity.

Of course, this particular renewal of the ancient law covenant was unique in that it was the final, perfecting renewal. It was *the* New Covenant. Its distinctiveness, according to Jeremiah's description of it, was that of fulfillment in contrast to the penultimate and imperfect nature of the Mosaic Covenant in all its previous renewals. This New Covenant would bring to pass the consummation of God's grace—consummation of divine revelation to men (vv. 33a, 34a), consummation of the personal relationship of God

---

[23] In Bultmann's formal reduction of the New Covenant to "a radically eschatological dimension, that is, a dimension outside the world" we have an example of an oversimplified appeal to Jer. 31:31ff. and similar biblical data in the interests of a metaphysic inhospitable to the biblical revelation of the New Covenant as historical ("Prophecy and Fulfillment" in *Essays on Old Testament Hermeneutics*, ed. C. Westermann [Richmond, 1963], [trans., J. C. G. Greig; originally in *Studia Theologica*, II (1949), 21-44], p. 63; cf. pp. 61f.). His dichotomy between historical and eschatological leaves no room for the biblical concept of a semi-eschatological age or community, just as it cannot accommodate a genuinely biblical concept of radical eschatology as historical consummation.

[24] *Cf.* J. Coppens, "La Nouvelle Alliance en Jer. 31, 31-34" in *The Catholic Biblical Quarterly*, 25, 1 (Jan., 1963), 12-21.

[25] Relevant here would be all that might be said of the New Testament's teaching that Jesus is a new and greater Moses. *Cf.* W. D. Davies, *The Setting of the Sermon on the Mount* (Cambridge, 1964), pp. 25ff.; T. F. Glasson, *Moses in the Fourth Gospel* (Naperville, 1963). Note also Jesus' fulfillment of the role of the Servant of the Lord, which in its individual aspect, and specifically in the area of lawgiving, reflects the figure of Moses.

to men in forgiveness and fellowship (vv. 33b, 34b).[26] But if the distinctiveness of the New Covenant is that of consummation, if when it abrogates it consummates, then its very discontinuity is expressive of its profound, organic unity with the Old Covenant.

Jeremiah speaks, to be sure, only of a consummation of grace; he does not mention a consummation of curses in the New Covenant. But the proper purpose of that covenant was, after all, salvation. Moreover, Jeremiah's particular concern was with the difference between the new and the old, and in respect of the visitation of covenant curses upon covenant members the New Covenant was not as clearly distinctive. Indeed, that aspect of covenant administration was particularly prominent in the Old Covenant, the divine wrath being at last visited upon the city of the Great King and upon the Old Testament people unto the uttermost.

Further, there is no reason to regard Jeremiah's description of the New Covenant as a comprehensive analysis, on the basis of which an exclusive judgment might then be rendered, excluding the curse sanction from a place in New Covenant administration. Even the aspect of New Covenant consummation that Jeremiah does deal with he views from the limited eschatological perspective of an Old Testament prophet. He beheld the messianic accomplishment in that perfection which historically is reached only in the fully eschatological age to come, as the ultimate goal of a process which in the present semi-eschatological age of this world is still marked by tragic imperfection. But the theologian of today ought not impose on himself the visionary limitations of an Old Testament prophet. By virtue of the fuller revelation he enjoys (*cf.* Lk. 10:24; I Pet. 1:10-12) he is able to distinguish these two distinct stages in the history of the New Covenant and to observe plainly that the imperfection of the covenant people and program has continued on from the Old Covenant into the present phase of New Covenant history. It is in accordance with this still only semi-eschatological state of affairs that the administration of the New Covenant is presently characterized by dual sanctions, having, in particular, anathemas to pronounce and excommunications

---

[26] Such is also the emphasis in the exposition of Jer. 31:31ff. in Hebrews. Because of the consummatory nature of the New Covenant some prefer not to classify it as a covenant renewal. *Cf.* B. W. Anderson, "The New Covenant and the Old" in *The Old Testament and Christian Faith* (New York, 1963), pp. 231f.; B. S. Childs, *Myth and Reality in the Old Testament* (Naperville, 1960), p. 79.

to execute.²⁷ To interpret Jeremiah's prophetic concept of the New Covenant as excluding curse sanctions is, therefore, to condemn it as fallacious.

Of incidental interest here is the understanding of the new covenant concept which is represented by the Qumran and Damascus covenanters when they set forth themselves as the community of the new covenant (1QpHab, II, 3; CDC, VI, 19; VIII, 21; XIX, 33f.; XX, 12). Especially significant for the question under discussion is the fact that these new covenant claimants continued the Mosaic covenant tradition of blessings and curses in an oath ritual of entrance (1QS, II, 4ff.; CDC, XV, 1ff.) and, consistently, had regulations for the excommunication of covenant breakers.²⁸

But the decisive and clear historical fact is that both blessing and curse are included in the administration of the true New Covenant. The Christ who stands like the theophanic ordeal pillar of fire in the midst of the seven churches addresses to them threats as well as promises, curses as well as blessings.²⁹ By his apostle he warns the Gentiles who are grafted into the tree of the covenant that just as Israelite branches had been broken off for their unbelief, they, too, if they failed to stand fast through faith, would not be spared (Rom. 11:17-21; *cf.* Matt. 8:12; John 15:1-8; Heb. 6:4ff.). Again, when the Lord appears in the final

---

²⁷ P. K. Jewett, while expressing a proper concern not to atrophy the movement of covenant history at some Old Testament stage, falls into the opposite error of prematurely precipitating the age to come. For when he defends a theology of baptism that bounds the rite and the covenant by faith, he anticipates the ultimate judicial separation into blessed faithful and accursed hypocrites of those who here and now, in the present semi-eschatological phase of the church's existence in this world, form the still undifferentiated mixed multitude of the covenant community. See his "Baptism (Baptist View)" in *The Encyclopedia of Christianity*, ed. E. H. Palmer (Wilmington, 1964), I, 524f.

Similarly, it is failure to reckon adequately with the only semi-eschatological character of the present administration of the New Covenant that vitiates R. E. O. White's critique of Marcel's use of the doctrine of the covenant in his discussion of baptism (*The Biblical Doctrine of Initiation* [Grand Rapids, 1960], pp. 286ff.).

²⁸ Moreover, the structure of the ancient treaties has been more broadly traced in sections of the Rule of the Community and of the Damascus Document (see Baltzer, *Das Bundesformular*, pp. 105-127).

²⁹ Rev. 2 and 3. Do we see in the figures of the messengers (angels) of the churches the messengers of the covenant lawsuit?

ordeal theophany as the Judge of the quick and the dead, taking fiery vengeance on them that obey not the gospel, he will bring before his judgment throne all who have been within his church of the New Covenant. There his declaration of the curse of the covenant will fall on the ears of some who in this world have been within the community that formally owns his covenant lordship, so that still in that day they think to cry, "Lord, Lord, have we not prophesied in thy name? and in thy name have cast out devils? and in thy name done many wonderful works?" (Matt. 7:21-23; *cf.* 13:24-30, 36-43, 47-49; 25:1-30; Rom. 14:10; II Cor. 5:10). There is, therefore, a fulfillment of the covenant lordship of Christ over his New Testament church unto condemnation and death as well as unto justification and life. In the execution of both verdicts, whether unto life or unto death, the New Covenant will be enforced and perfected.

We are bound to conclude, therefore, that the newness of the New Covenant cannot involve the elimination of the curse sanction as a component of the covenant and that this newness consequently poses no problem for the interpretation of Christian baptism as a sign of ordeal embracive of both blessing and curse. In confirmation of this conclusion we may recall that John the Baptist analyzed the work of the coming One as a baptism of judgment in the Holy Spirit and fire. Christ so baptized the Mosaic covenant community, and he so baptizes the congregation of the New Covenant.

Pentecost belongs to both the old and new orders. It was the beginning of the messianic ordeal visited on the Mosaic community. Those who received that baptism of Pentecost emerged vindicated as the people of the New Covenant, the inheritors of the kingdom. Pentecost was thus a baptismal ordeal in Spirit and fire in which redemptive covenant realized its proper end (*cf.* Acts 1:5). But the Israel of that generation which did not share in this baptism of justification soon experienced the messianic baptism as a judgment curse unto death, destruction, and dispersion. So also the semi-eschatological phase of the New Covenant moves on towards a messianic ordeal which will bring for the justified meek the inheritance of the earth, but judicial exposure and the curse-sentence of excision for the apostates. As an Old Testament prophet, even though standing at the threshold of the messianic kingdom, John did not distinguish these distinct moments in the messianic baptism ordeal. But we who are within the kingdom of God perceive that John's own water ritual pointed to the ordeal of Israel, while the Christian rite that bears the name and continues the essential form of John's baptism signifies the rapidly approaching ordeal appointment of the people of the New Covenant.

Conclusions: Christian baptism is a sign of the eschatological ordeal in which the Lord of the covenant brings his servants to account. In baptismal contexts this judgment is often viewed more specifically as that through which the Christian passes in Christ, in whose ordeal the final judgment of the elect was intruded into mid-history. That is, judgment is viewed in such cases only in so far as it involves the specific verdict of justification. Agreeably, the import of the baptismal sign of judgment is then expounded in soteriological terms like regeneration, sanctification, incorporation by the Holy Spirit into the body of Christ, or protective sealing against the day of wrath. But even when the consideration of baptism is thus restricted to its significance for the elect, judgment as curse and death remains at the center of baptism's import and continues to be the specific object of its symbolic portrayal. For the blessing of the elect arises only out of their Saviour's accursed death.

One's theology of the sacramental signs of the covenant will have to be consistent with his theology of the covenant itself. If the covenant concept is constricted to an administration of grace to the elect, then it will hardly seem possible that the signs marking entrance into the covenant should signify a judicial consummation of the covenant which is fraught with ultimate curse as well as ultimate blessing. It has appeared, however, that there is independent evidence available for interpreting these signs of incorporation as signifying the dual covenant sanctions; and this provides, then, yet further proof of the impossibility of satisfying all the biblical data with the restricted, guaranteed-promise conception of covenant. It is also another confirmation of the necessity of making the idea of God's lordship the central focus of the systematic doctrine of covenant.

Now if the covenant is first and last a declaration of God's lordship, then the baptismal sign of entrance into it will before all other things be a sign of coming under the jurisdiction of the covenant and particularly under the covenantal dominion of the Lord. Christian baptism is thus the New Covenant sign of consecration or discipleship.

It is immediately evident in the great commission (Matt. 28:18-20) that consignment under the authority of Christ is the chief thing in Christian baptism. For there baptizing the nations takes its place alongside teaching them to obey Christ's commandments in specification of the charge to disciple them to him who has been given all authority in heaven and earth.[30] Of similar significance are a concatenation like Paul's "one Lord, one faith, one baptism" (Eph. 4:5) and the common confession of Jesus as Lord or Christ in baptismal formulae (Acts 2:38; 8:16; 19:5; I Cor. 1:13ff.; *cf.* I Pet. 3:21; Rom. 10:9).[31] The related baptismal phraseology of "in (or into) the name of Jesus Christ" (or "of the Lord," or of the Trinity) also expresses the nature of baptism as confirmation of an authority or ownership relationship, judging from analogous usage in the Old Testament[32] and in Hellenistic legal and commercial papyri.[33] Further evidence is the representation of baptism as a seal, in the sense of a token of authority or mark of ownership.[34] According to the New Testament emphasis on the proper soteric purpose of redemptive covenant, the seal motif may be used as an assurance to believers of their security in the hour of eschatological crisis (Eph. 1:13f.; 4:30; II Tim. 2:19; Rev. 7:2ff.; 14:1; 22:4). But baptism is to be more comprehensively understood as a sealing with the name of the Trinity invoked in the consecration oath in recognition that the triune Lord is God of the covenant oath and its dual sanctions.

The incorporation of disciples into the jurisdiction of the New Covenant by the baptismal confession of Christ as Lord is in clear continuity with the tradition of the initiatory oath of allegiance found in Old Testament covenantal engagements (and their extra-biblical counterparts).[35] Comparable also are the initiatory

---

[30] Note also the interrelationship of baptizing and making disciples in John 4:1.

[31] According to certain form-critical studies much in the way of New Testament confessional formulation had its source in baptismal liturgy. Some of the more extreme conclusions of this type are yielding to analyses that recognize a greater complexity of origin. *Cf.* Vernon H. Neufeld, *The Earliest Christian Confessions* (Grand Rapids, 1963), pp. 6ff.

[32] *E.g.*, Deut. 28:9, 10; Isa. 63:19.

[33] *Cf.* W. F. Arndt and F. W. Gingrich, *A Greek-English Lexicon of the New Testament and Other Early Christian Literature* (Chicago and Cambridge, 1957), p. 575. See also our remarks above on I Cor. 10:2.

[34] *Cf.* G. W. H. Lampe, *The Seal of the Spirit* (London, New York, Toronto, 1951), pp. 8-18.

[35] See the discussion of I Pet. 3:21 above. In connection with I Cor. 11:27 and Heb. 10:26-31, G. E. Mendenhall notes the continuity between

oaths which were required by the Essenes, according to Josephus,[36] and at Qumran (1QS, I, 16ff.; V, 8ff.), for entrance into the covenant.[37]

As an oath-sign of allegiance to Christ the Lord, baptism is a sacrament in the original sense of *sacramentum* in its etymological relation to the idea of consecration, and more particularly in its employment for the military oath of allegiance.[38] And if the immediate function of baptism in covenant administration is to serve as the ritual of an oath of discipleship, we have in that another indication that baptism is a symbolic portrayal of the judgment of the covenant. For, as we have seen, covenant oath rituals were enactments of the sanctions invoked in the oath. Indeed, from these historic antecedents we may infer that baptism as an oath ritual symbolizes in particular the curse sanction, the death judgment threatened in the covenant.[39] To say that baptism portrays the covenant curse is not to say that baptism as a sign of trial by ordeal signifies only an unfavorable verdict. For as we have previously observed in connection with both circumcision and baptism, the curse of the ordeal may be suffered by the forsworn in himself, but it is undergone by the elect as a soteric experience in their identification with the Redeemer.

The foregoing analyses bear out the contention that there is a thoroughgoing correspondence between the meaning of baptism and that of circumcision. Both are confessional oath-signs of consecration to the Lord of the covenant, and both signify his ultimate redemptive judgment with its potential of both condemnation and justification. There is indeed a shift in emphasis from the malediction side of the judgment spectrum to the vindication side as covenant revelation moves on from Old Testament cir-

---

the significance of the cup of the New Covenant sacrament of the Lord's Supper and the Mosaic tradition of covenant oath and curse ("Covenant" in *The Interpreter's Dictionary of the Bible* [Nashville, 1962], p. 722).

[36] *Wars*, II, 8, 7f.

[37] For the self-maledictory character of these oaths, see 1QS, V, 12 (*cf.* II, 4ff.).

[38] *Cf.* Pliny's use of *sacramentum* to denote the oath taken by Christians in their worship, binding themselves to abstain from certain sins (*Letters*, X, 96). Early baptismal liturgy and comments thereon commonly expound the rite as an engagement to serve God and as a renunciation of Satan. *Cf.* I Tim. 6:12.

[39] See the Hittite Soldiers' Oath in *Ancient Near Eastern Texts*, ed. Pritchard (Princeton, 1950), pp. 353f. *Cf.* our discussion of circumcision above.

cumcision to New Testament baptism (the baptism of John being in this respect, too, transitional). This change reflects the movement of redemptive history from an administration of condemnation to one of righteousness. Nevertheless, the maledictory element is no more to be excluded from the New Testament sign of consecration because of this shift in emphasis than vindication-qualification is to be excluded from the meaning of the Old Testament rite simply because that was characteristically an administration of condemnation and death.

The form and name of baptism are enough to prevent such an oversimplification of its complex meaning. The form, as we have seen, symbolizes a visitation of judgment waters, and, as its name indicates, the ritual proper does not comprise the emergence of the baptized person from the water but only his entrance into the symbolic judgment. For on no view of the meaning of $\beta\alpha\pi\tau\acute{\iota}\zeta\omega$ is any thought of emergence involved. In fact, the metaphorical meaning that it develops is that of perishing.[40] At the same time there is no contradiction between the form or name of the sign and the soteric aspect of baptism's significance, which is emphasized in the New Testament. For even though the waters portray the judgment curse, the rite does not prejudge the ultimate issue of the individual's destiny one way or the other. It places him under the authority of the Lord for judgment and tells him that as a sinner he must pass through the curse; yet it also calls him to union with his Lord, promising to all who are found in Christ a safe passage through the curse waters of the ordeal.

A further word on the relevance of the foregoing for the question of the mode of administering baptism is in order. As for the meaning of $\beta\alpha\pi\tau\acute{\iota}\zeta\omega$, its semantic development evidently proceeded from the primary idea of dipping in water to secondary metaphorical ideas like overwhelm and (in the Scriptures) to the secondary special idea of administering a religious water rite. Then from the particular significance of certain of these sacred rituals as signs of ordeal (and perhaps with an assist from the metaphorical meaning of overwhelm, which was common in the usage of the Greek world) $\beta\alpha\pi\tau\acute{\iota}\zeta\omega$ came to be used in the Bible

---

[40] This warns against the common but unwarranted attempt to trace a complete modal parallel between the baptismal action and the death-burial-resurrection pattern of Christ's ordeal. *Cf.* further John Murray, *Christian Baptism* (Philadelphia, 1952), pp. 29-33; R. Schnackenburg, *op. cit.*, pp. 55ff., 67ff.

for the idea of undergoing a judgment ordeal, whether or not by water. If this analysis is in the main correct, it is academic to debate the contention that the idea of immersion belongs inseparably to the primary meaning of βαπτίζω. Further, any exclusivistic claims for the sole propriety of some one mode of administering baptism are gratuitous. For any mode of relating the water to a person that is attested in the various biblical water ordeals would have biblical warrant. Of course, not all such modes would prove expedient. In Israel's passage through the Red Sea the baptismal waters stood in a threatening (if actually protective) position over against the Israelites without, however, touching them, while in the Jordan crossing, the waters were so far removed as to be quite out of sight. At the other extreme, Jonah, like the accused in the Babylonian water ordeal, was plunged into the depths (not to mention now his novel conveyance), and the baptized family in the Noahic deluge ordeal sailed over the rising flood while torrents descended from above.[41]

If this means on the one hand that no exclusive claims can be made for the mode of immersion, it would nevertheless appear that the symbolic aptness of that mode remains unimpaired by the interpretation of baptism as a sign of judgment. Baptism by immersion will surely impress many as a most eloquent way of portraying the great judgment of God, while the familiar imposition of moistened finger tips which is generously called sprinkling must seem to many to project quite inadequately the threatening power and crisis of the ultimate ordeal.[42] Is it not time for Reformed liturgists to address themselves to the task of finding a form for the baptismal sign which, while suitable for the very young and the frail, will capture and convey something of the decisive encounter which baptism signifies?[43]

[41] It was noted earlier that in the witness of John the Baptist the messianic baptism with the Holy Spirit and fire was to be understood as an ordeal. The coming of the Spirit by an affusion at Pentecost may, therefore, be cited as a modal variety of baptismal ordeal.

[42] Since the idea of qualification in the specific form of cleansing is included in the import of baptism (*cf.*, *e.g.*, Eph. 5:26; Tit. 3:5; Acts 22:16) it might seem desirable to practice a mode of baptism suggestive of washing as well as ordeal. To that extent, appeals to ritual cleansing techniques such as sprinkling would have some relevance.

[43] F. W. Dillistone calls it "one of the most urgent tasks of our day" to revitalize the potentially profound appeal of this water symbol within the Christian community (*Christianity and Symbolism* [Philadelphia, 1955], p. 187; *cf.* pp. 215f.).

CHAPTER SIX

THE ADMINISTRATION OF CIRCUMCISION AND BAPTISM

The Covenant of Redemption is an administration of God's kingdom. It is an institutional embodiment of the divine lordship in an earthly community. The question arises, then, as to how this divine authority structure relates itself to other coexisting authority structures. At present we are concerned with this matter in so far as it may involve principles relevant to the administration of the covenantal oath-signs of consecration. In turning to this aspect of our study of circumcision and baptism, we will once again try to sharpen our historical perspective by viewing the divine covenants against the background of their formal counterparts in the ancient world.

I. VASSAL AUTHORITY IN COVENANT ADMINISTRATION

The suzerain-vassal covenants were authority structures which brought outlying spheres of authority under the sanctioned control of an imperial power. The great king gave his treaty to a vassal who was himself also a king. In imposing his covenant the suzerain did not dissolve the royal authority of his vassal, as an empire builder would in the case of the territorial annexation of another kingdom as a province. Indeed, it was precisely in his status as a king that the vassal was addressed in the treaty. The dynastic succession within the vassal kingdom was sometimes a matter of explicit concern in the treaty stipulations. The historical prologue of the treaty might reflect on the fact that it was the suzerain's efforts that had established the vassal king on his throne; more than that, the covenant itself was at times the very means of his doing so. It was then by swearing the vassal's oath of allegiance that a throne aspirant became king or a king was re-established in his dominion over his people. There is even evidence that the treaty could be the means of enlarging a vassal king's domain.[1]

It is of course obvious from the whole purpose of these treaties that the vassal king in taking the ratificatory oath did so in his capacity as king and thus brought his kingdom with him into the relationship of allegiance to the suzerain. Moreover, from express statements in the treaties we know that the vassal king assumed responsibility for his sons and more remote descendants, consigning them with himself in his covenant oath. Consequently, these descendants are mentioned in the curses as objects of divine vengeance if the covenant sworn by the vassal king should be broken.

A few examples may be cited. The treaty of Esarhaddon with Ramataia begins:

> The treaty which Esarhaddon, king of the world, king of Assyria, son of Sennacherib, likewise king of the world, king of Assyria, with Ramataia, city-ruler of Urakazabanu, with his sons, his grandsons, with all the Urakazabaneans young and old, as many as there be—with (all of) you, your sons, your grandsons who will exist in days to come after the treaty, from sunrise to sunset, over as many as Esarhaddon, king of Assyria, exercises kingship and lordship—(so) he has made the treaty with you concerning Ashurbanipal, the crown-prince, son of Esarhaddon, king of Assyria.[2]

Later in this same treaty Ramataia is reminded:

> [Esarhaddon] has made you take an oath that you will relate [the treaty-provisions] to your sons and to your grandsons, to your seed, to your seed's seed which shall be (born) in the future, that you will order them as follows: —"Guard this treaty. Do not transgress your treaty, (or) you will lose your lives, you

[1] *Cf.* McCarthy, *Treaty and Covenant*, pp. 83-91; J. M. Munn-Rankin, "Diplomacy in Western Asia in the Early Second Millennium B.C.," *Iraq*, 18 (1956), 68-110.

[2] Col. 1:1-12. The translation is that of D. J. Wiseman in *The Vassal-Treaties of Esarhaddon*, p. 30. For a similar formula in biblical covenant administration see Deut. 29:9-14 (10-15). *Cf.* also the language of Peter in Acts 2:39; *cf.* v. 17.

will be turning over your dwellings to be shattered, your people to be carried off."³

The Sefireh treaty begins:

The treaty of Bar-ga'ayah, king of KTK, with Mati'el, son of 'Attarsamak, king [of Arpad; and the trea]ty of the sons of Bar-ga'ayah with the sons of Mati'el; and the treaty of the grandsons of Bar-ga'aya[h and] his [descendants] with the descendants of Mati'el.⁴

The concluding curse of the treaty between the Hittite Mursilis and Duppi-Tessub of Amurru reads:

The words of the treaty and the oath that are inscribed on this tablet—should Duppi-Tessub not honor these words of the treaty and the oath, may these gods of the oath destroy Duppi-Tessub together with his person, his wife, his son, his grandson, his house, his land and together with everything that he owns.⁵

It is clear, then, that these ancient treaties, on the form of which the redemptive covenants were patterned, were engagements not merely between individuals but between broader authority structures. In particular, the servant king who was bound by the treaty was bound not alone but together with his subjects and his descendants.

II. CIRCUMCISION AND GENERATION

From the pervasive formal correspondence between the divine covenants and the international vassal treaties it would be reasonable to infer that in the covenant of circumcision, too, the chief vassal figure was approached not in abstraction from his authority status but with his societal station in view, being confronted with the demand to subject all within his sphere of authority to that higher authority before which he was himself summoned to bow the knee. We are not dependent, however, solely on such inference, for analysis of the direct scriptural evidence leads us to the same conclusion.

³ Col. 4:287-295. See Wiseman, *op. cit.*, pp. 49ff.

⁴ I, A, 1ff. The translation is that given in McCarthy, *op. cit.*, p. 189.

⁵ The translation is that of A. Goetze in *Ancient Near Eastern Texts*, p. 205.

One aspect of the circumcision rite not considered above has direct relevance here. The fact that circumcision was performed on an organ of generation is surely meant to indicate that the significance of the rite—both as a sign of malediction and of consecration—had reference to the descendants of the vassal who swore the circumcision oath-curse.

Supplementing what we have concluded as to the primary oath-curse meaning of circumcision, we may now add that the specific malediction expressed by the symbolic action of circumcising the foreskin was the cutting off of the vassal's descendants so as to leave him without heir or name in the kingdom. In the parallel extra-biblical treaties there are numerous instances of the particular curse of being denied offspring or having one's descendants cut off. The following examples come from Esarhaddon's treaty with Ramataia. "May he [Ashur] never grant you fatherhood" (col. 6=415f.). "[May Ṣarpanitu who gives] name and seed, destroy your name and your seed [from the land]" (col. 6=435f.). "[Just as the seed of] a hinney [is sterile,] [may your name,] your seed and the seed of [your sons] and your [daughters be destroyed] from the land" (col. 7=537-539).[6] A curse against the one who violated the treaty of Ashurnirari V with Mati'ilu was that he might "be a mule" and "his wife [have no] offspring."[7] The treaty-deed of Abban with Iarimlim concludes with this curse against any who would alter Abban's deed: "May Ishtar who makes eunuchs . . . bind his member" (1. 19f.).[8] The final curse in the treaty of Tudhaliyas IV and Ulmi-Teshub is that if anyone changes even a word of the treaty tablet, "may . . . the thousand gods of this tablet root that man's descendants out of the land of Hatti" (rev. 25ff.).[9]

In this common treaty-curse there was the perfect foil for the blessing that was so prominent in the covenant of circumcision, the blessing of the promised son for Abraham and Sarah. And this precise opposition that obtains between the particular blessing that is dominant in the Genesis 17 context and the circumcision-curse as we have interpreted it becomes convincing proof of the correctness of that interpretation when we observe that such an exact matching of curses and blessings is characteristic

---

[6] *Cf.* Wiseman, *op. cit.*, pp. 60, 62, 70. The first example quoted is the first specific curse in the lengthy curse section of this treaty.

[7] Col. 5. *Cf.* McCarthy, *op. cit.*, p. 196.

[8] *Cf.* D. J. Wiseman, *The Alalakh Tablets* (London, 1953), p. 25.

[9] *Cf.* McCarthy, *op. cit.*, p. 185.

of the sanctions of the second millennium treaties. For a biblical example, see in the Deuteronomic treaty the pairing of the sixfold blessing of 28:3-6 and the sixfold curse of 28:16-19, and note especially the appearance there again of the particular curse-blessing contrast featured in the covenant of circumcision: "cursed [or blessed] shall be the fruit of thy body" (vv. 4 and 18).

But the circumcision oath-rite was also a sign of consecration, and in relation to that the meaning of the application of the circumcision sign to the male organ of generation would be that the descendants of the circumcised were consecrated with him to the Lord of the covenant. Corresponding to this was God's promissory definition of this covenant as one he would establish with Abraham's descendants after him (Gen. 17:7). What may be inferred from the nature of circumcision as a cutting off of the foreskin is more explicitly expressed by the prescription of Genesis 17 that circumcision was to be administered (not only at the initial ratification ceremony of that day but throughout the coming generations) to the vassal's sons, and that on their eighth day (v. 12). Thus the vassal's descendants, who yet unborn were consecrated in the circumcision of their forefathers, were again and individually consecrated by the direct application of the sign of consecration to themselves.

These regulations for the administration of circumcision reveal the Abrahamic Covenant to be, like other vassal covenants, an instrument for incorporating a whole authority unit within the higher jurisdiction of the covenant suzerain. Nor was the authority unit in question confined to the sphere of Abraham's parental authority. He was instructed to bring the servants of his house as well as his son Ishmael under the sign of Yahweh's authority (vv. 12f., 23, 27). The vassal unit thus extended to the more comprehensive sphere comprised within Abraham's authority as parent-householder.

The principle emerges here that a man who enters God's covenant by personal confession is held responsible by his Lord to bind with himself under the yoke of the covenant certain others of his subordinates (as more precisely specified in the stipulations of a particular covenant administration). To fail to do so is a contradiction of one's oath of allegiance. That is why Moses, for the uncircumcision of his son, was in peril of the curse that was invoked against him in his own circumcision (Ex. 4:24-26).[10] The

---

[10] A recent challenge to the traditional understanding of this passage as involving a threat against the life of Moses is presented by H. Kosmala

verses immediately preceding that episode record God's commission to Moses to demand of Pharaoh that he let God's covenant son Israel go to serve him (Ex. 4:21-23). But how could Moses be the bearer of such a demand, how could he be the minister of God to lead forth the multitude of the Lord's servant-sons to their great consecration act at the mount of God, when he had neglected to consecrate his own son to the Lord by circumcision? So it was that God threatened to cut him off from his destiny in Israel—like the accursed ram in the Assyrian ratification ritual cited earlier, separated from the herd, never again to return to its place at their head.[11]

We conclude, then, that the principle of vassal authority was integral to the administration of circumcision as sign of entrance into God's redemptive covenant. Confession of Yahweh's lordship as a matter of personal faith constituted the necessary nucleus and historical beginning for the administration of the rite, and thus for the formal establishment of the covenant community for which circumcision was (paradoxically) the sign of inclusion. There had to be an Abraham. But Abraham could not enter into this oath and covenant simply as an individual. It was Abraham the parent-householder, Abraham the patriarch, to whom God gave the covenant of circumcision. In keeping with the nature of the covenant as that may be discerned in the light of the most relevant biblical and extra-biblical data, covenantal incorporation into the kingdom of God did not proceed exclusively in terms of individual confession. The formation of the ancient covenant community was rather a process of incorporating households which were under the authority of a confessing servant of the Lord.

("The 'Bloody Husband'" in *Vetus Testamentum*, 12 [1962], 14-28). Taking the pericope (Ex. 4:24-26) by itself, he is able to offer a plausible interpretation of the unaltered consonantal text in terms of a threat against a son of Moses, Moses himself not figuring at all in the episode. Several of the elements of Kosmala's exegesis seem sound; yet, as he acknowledges himself (p. 15), the passage according to the context in which it comes to us concerns a divine threat against the life of Moses.

[11] So understood, this seemingly abrupt intrusion into Exodus 4 has clear thematic relevance for its context. Also, the blood-smearing rite performed by Zipporah to avert the threatening death (v. 25b) invites comparison with the similar feature in the original passover ritual (Ex. 12:7, 22), the occasion of which is mentioned in the divine warning cited immediately before the pericope under discussion (see Ex. 4:23).

III. THE AUTHORITY PRINCIPLE AND BAPTISM

When covenant is no longer identified with election and guaranteed blessing, and especially when the baptismal sign of incorporation into the covenant is understood as pointing without prejudice to a judgment ordeal with the potential of both curse and blessing, certain questions that have long ensnarled the polemics of infant baptism are eliminated from consideration as no longer relevant. Within the framework of the approach to covenant and baptism being developed here, the practice of infant baptism would clearly involve no presumption that the children of believers are Christians by birth.[12] No theory of presumptive regeneration as the basis for the administration of baptism to infants could be reared on the foundation of law covenant. Neither, on our approach, would the baptism of the infants of believers signify a divine promise that they were destined to secure the blessings of the covenant sooner or later. Hence, there would be no need to theorize how the baptism of such might serve as a means of conveying to them the grace supposedly sealed to them by the rite, much less to apologize for the numerous cases in which that grace never is conveyed.

---

[12] Contesting the paedobaptist's appeal to the correspondence of baptism with circumcision, P. K. Jewett writes: "he reads the OT concept of a literal seed into the NT and argues that his children are Christians and members of the church by birth, with a right to baptism, just as in the OT a man was born a Jew with the right to circumcision as a citizen of the OT Jewish theocracy" (*The Encyclopedia of Christianity*, p. 525). According to Jewett, the paedobaptist does this because of his failure to observe that while the Jews possessed a terrestrial version of the celestial inheritance, "this temporal and terrestrial aspect of the covenant blessing has now passed away" (*ibid.*, p. 524). The irrelevance of this type of argument for the view of covenant and baptism which the present article advocates is noted above. Here we would question the accuracy of the analysis of the difference between the historical contexts of circumcision and baptism. Since the theocracy in the kingdom form which Jewett evidently has in view came into being long after circumcision was instituted, is it not misleading to identify a Jew's right to circumcision with his citizenship in the theocratic kingdom? For over the first half-millennium of the administration of circumcision those who received it did not possess a temporal-terrestrial kingdom. Actually, there is in this very respect a remarkable similarity between the age of Abraham when the covenant of circumcision was given and our New Testament age. Then as now the saints had promises of a kingdom of glory but were obliged to wait for the manifestation of it in any form whatsoever, temporal or eternal. In fact, the patriarchs were never to receive it in any other form than we Christians do, namely, as the eternal new heaven and new earth.

For us the pertinent question is whether the covenant for which baptism serves as oath-sign of incorporation is, like the divine covenants of the Old Testament and the parallel vassal covenants of the ancient world, a relationship of authority spheres rather than simply of individuals. That the New Covenant is in this respect like its precursors would be the natural inference to draw from our analysis of the New Covenant as generically one with the earlier covenants, new and old being alike law covenants, declarations of God's lordship over a people bound to him under the sanctions of life and death.[13] The pattern of authority is not peripheral but central in the vassal covenant form, and therefore the whole weight of the historical case for identifying the New Covenant as a continuation of the earlier Suzerain-vassal covenants presses for the conclusion that this New Covenant is administered to confessors not just as individuals but as heads of authority units.

Direct New Testament evidence is available to the effect that Christ's authority as Lord of the covenant does indeed extend to his disciples' subordinates, commanding their obedience. At least that can be shown to be true in the case of the children of believers.

The statement of Paul in I Corinthians 7:14 is sufficiently problematic to recommend caution in polemical appeal to it, but some account of it must be ventured. There would have to be general agreement that according to this passage Paul's definition of religious status was not determined by exclusively individualistic criteria. In line with certain Old Testament categories of thought, he predicated with respect to the New Testament situation a species of sanctification that obtains not necessarily in union with personal faith (thinking now of the children) and even in spite of personal unbelief (thinking here of the non-Christian parent) and only by reason of a cultural (specifically, social) relationship sustained to a believer.

Treating first the case of the children of the mixed marriages under discussion by the apostle, there does not seem to be any way to construe the holiness ascribed to them other than as a holiness of status. There can be no question here, as there is in the case of the sanctification of the unbelieving parent, whether the holiness might be not stative but active or functional. In what, then, does the holiness of the children's status consist? In accord-

---

[13] See above, under "New Covenant Judgment" in Chapter Five.

ance with the biblical concept of holiness it will have to involve some sort of dedicatory separation unto the name of God, a consecration to his service and glory. Clearly it is not the holy consecration of subjective-spiritual condition, nor is it that of the sacred symbol. To come to a positive conclusion requires a look at the Old Testament background of the conception of holiness here utilized by Paul.

In the Old Testament theocracy there was a blending of cultural (*i.e.*, covenantal) and cultic models to describe the religious relationship of Israel to the Lord. Israel was made unto God "a kingdom of priests, and a holy nation" (Ex. 19:6). The holy sanctuary of Israel's God was one with the throne room of the Great King of Israel's covenant.[14] In this integration of priestly and political figures, cultic affiliation (or holiness) and covenantal allegiance were equivalents. Both alike were expressive of formal consecration into the special community of God's people.

It can only be such a holiness of inclusion within the covenant community that is attributed to the children in I Corinthians 7:14. That Paul should regard the holiness of the believing parent as involving the holiness of the children is in keeping with the Old Testament law of holiness as Paul himself elsewhere expounds it, and that with reference to this very matter of the status of the descendants of covenant members: "If the dough offered as first fruits is holy, so is the whole lump; and if the root is holy, so are the branches" (Rom. 11:16, RSV; *cf.* Num. 15:20).[15] Beyond this general teaching of Romans 11, the peculiar point of I Corinthians 7:14 is that the extension of this holiness to a new generation requires no more than one believing parent, the sacred prevailing over the profane in such a case.

Corresponding to the genealogical extension of cultic holiness

[14] Attention was directed above (Chapter One) to the way in which covenant ratification rite and cultic sacrifice merged in the Sinaitic ceremonies.

[15] Beasley-Murray (*Baptism in the New Testament*, pp. 194-196) traces the holiness of I Cor. 7:14 to its proper source. He fails, however, to do justice to the equivalence of this holiness and covenant membership in Romans 11, evidently because he misunderstands that passage to teach that unbelieving Jews continue through the Christian era in the holy status of branches derived from the holy root. This interpretation overlooks the implications of the radical historical development described as the breaking off of the unbelieving branches (Rom. 11:17ff.). More serious still, Beasley-Murray would dismiss this concept of holiness from normative Christian thought by the evasive plea that it is not characteristic of Paul or of the New Testament generally.

there is in the analogous political model of God's people the extension of the covenant rule in terms of the vassal authority principle. These are two modes of describing the same reality. Since I Corinthians 7:14 provides evidence that the cultic corollary of the authority principle was operative in the apostolic church, this passage may be cited in support of the thesis that the authority principle is still in effect in the administration of the New Covenant, at least in the form of parental authority.

According to I Corinthians 7:14 the unbelieving spouse also participates somehow in cultic holiness. If this participation had to be understood in precisely the same way as that of the children, then we should have to regard such persons as belonging within the covenant community. If that were so, it would be necessary to recognize the extension of cultic holiness through the marriage relationship to an unbelieving partner as constituting a third principle of covenant inclusion alongside personal confession and the authority principle. For the principle of cultic holiness would apply in a relationship where the authority principle was not applicable inasmuch as this holiness might extend through the wife to the husband.

But while the similarity of terminology in verse 14a and 14b of I Corinthians 7 requires that the sanctification be of the same kind (*i.e.*, cultic) in the case of the unbelieving parents and of the children, it is an unjustifiably wooden approach to the apostle's words that insists that this cultic sanctification must apply in exactly the same manner in the two cases. Rather than think of sanctification of status in the case of the unbelieving parents it is possible and, it seems, preferable to understand that their holiness, which Paul describes as possessed in the believing spouse, is a sanctification of these unbelievers in the functioning of the marriage relationship and particularly in that role which fulfills the central and distinctive purpose of marriage. In effect, the force of the language is then that the marriage relationship itself was sanctified by virtue of the presence of the believer unto the service of the holy covenant of God and specifically unto the securing of a holy seed.

In the discussion of infant baptism the episode of the bringing of the children to Jesus (Matt. 19:13-15; Mk. 10:13-16; Lk. 18:15-17) has been the source of considerable contention. But in support of the point we would make we need gather no more from that episode than that our Lord heartily approved when those with parental authority over these children exercised it to bring them to him and place them under the authority of his ministry. And that much at least would seem to be beyond debate. Another significant fact is that Paul instructed the children of various congregations to obey their parents in the Lord, and in support of his charge cited the pertinent stipulation of the Sinaitic Covenant together with its accompanying covenantal sanction (Eph. 6:1-3; Col. 3:20; *cf.* Ex. 20:12). Clear confirmation is also found in Paul's directive to covenant parents to bring their children under the nurturing and admonishing authority of the Lord (Eph. 6:4). In this exhortation the apostle takes for granted that it is the very authority of Christ as covenant Lord that reaches and claims children through the authority of their parents.

It is therefore a matter of express scriptural teaching that the disciple of Christ is bound to bring those who are under his parental authority along with himself when he comes by oath under the higher authority of his covenant Suzerain. From this it follows that the Scriptures provide ample warrant for the administration of baptism to the children of confessing Christians, for baptism is the New Covenant rite whose precise significance is that of committal to Christ's authority and of incorporation within the domain of Christ's covenant lordship.[16]

While the New Testament thus indicates decisively that the independent authority of the covenant servant continues to be a regulative factor in covenant administration, the explicit evidence for this is confined to the authority of the parent over his children. There does not appear to be unambiguous evidence in the New Testament that either the marital institution with the husband's authority over the wife or the societal authority structure of master and servant has been taken up into the organizational structure of the New Covenant. On the contrary, there are indications in the New Testament that at least in the case of marital authority the old administrative policy has been changed.

Under the Old Covenant, although the wives did not receive a sign of entrance into the covenant, they were none the less brought within the rule of the covenant along with the children and household servants when their husbands entered the covenant (*cf., e.g.,* Deut. 29:10ff.; Neh. 10:28f.; Gen. 35:2ff.). Whatever their personal religious attitude, as members of a covenant member's household the wives were under the authority and sanctions of the covenant Lord. The idea might not be enter-

---

[16] See above, Chapter Five, under "Conclusions."

tained by one of the patriarchs or by a later Israelite that he was at liberty to permit his wife to dissociate herself from the covenantal relationship to which he had bound himself. The demand made in the reforms of Ezra and Nehemiah that the Israelites put away their foreign wives (Ezra 9:1ff.; Neh. 13:23ff.) was not really a contradiction of this. For the inception of these marriages was judged to have been in violation of prior covenantal regulations (see especially verse 30 in the Nehemiah 10 record of Israel's oath-curse of covenant renewal), and therefore any sincere purpose to restore true submission to Yahweh's authority must include the termination of these covenant-breaking marital alliances.[17]

The New Testament did not cancel the requirement that covenant members marry within the covenant; it is in the Lord that they are still to marry (I Cor. 7:39). But the expanding missions situation to which the pages of the New Testament were addressed produced a mixed-marriage problem of a different complexion from that dealt with by Ezra and Nehemiah and one, therefore, to be handled in a different way (see I Cor. 7:12ff.). Paul's solution calling for the preservation of the marriage, unless the unbeliever initiated a separation, was based on the prevailing power of divine grace. The fact that divorce in this situation though not mandatory was permissible within the stipulated conditions reflects the New Testament apostle's fundamental agreement on covenantal priorities with the post-exilic Israelite reformers. But what we are especially concerned to observe in this connection is that if the Corinthian Christians had looked on the unbelieving spouses who were willing to live with their Christian partners as though they, too, belonged to the covenant community, and particularly, if these unbelievers had received the baptismal sign of church membership, it would scarcely be possible to account for the rise among these Corinthians of doubt as to whether these marriages ought to be continued. We may gather, then, from the implications of I Corinthians 7 that the believing husband's marital authority is not to be regarded under the New Covenant as being at the same time a covenantal authority that claims his wife for the church.

---

[17] Later Jewish practice indulged in the casuistry of subjecting a slave woman coercively to a baptismal ritual that would qualify her for marriage to a Jewish master. *Cf.* Strack and Billerbeck, *Kommentar zum Neuen Testament aus Talmud und Midrasch*, I, 1054f. My attention was called to this by Helmuth Egelkraut.

Although the slave shares with the wife in the significant feature of responsible adulthood, the important differences between these two household positions (particularly in societal contexts where the wife had been delivered from household-property status) must give us some pause in using our conclusions concerning the church relationship of the Christian's unbelieving wife to support a similarly negative conclusion on the covenantal status of a Christian master's slave who has not yet confessed faith in Christ. For one thing, the slave is not legally free to register his religious indecision or dissent by leaving the master's household. And there is no apostolic word to Christian masters concerning such servants corresponding to Paul's advice to Christian husbands to let their unbelieving wives who were so minded depart. In certain respects, therefore, the master-servant relationship is more akin to the parent-child authority structure than to that of husband and wife. The question is in order, then, whether the master-servant relationship was, in continuation of Old Testament practice,[18] taken up along with the parent-child relationship into the authority structure of the New Covenant.

It would be possible to interpret the New Testament accounts of household baptisms in and of themselves as involving the baptism of household servants along with their converted masters, and indeed on the basis of the confession of the latter (Acts 16:15, 33f.; I Cor. 1:16; *cf.* Acts 2:38f.; 10:2, 47f.; 11:14; 18:8; II Tim. 1:16; 4:19; John 4:53). There are, however, other plausible interpretations of these episodes. Without, therefore, entering again here into a detailed discussion of these indecisive passages[19] we would simply observe that for the purpose of substantiating the

---

[18] On the late continuation of the Abrahamic precedent (Gen. 17) see the Damascus Document 12:11 and *cf.* Strack and Billerbeck, *op. cit.*, IV, 722ff. Noteworthy is the option of the non-Jewish slave to persist in an uncircumcised state through a period of deliberation, with subsequent resale to a non-Jewish master. One might expect at least as much tolerance in New Testament practice, especially since the pressure for religious conformity produced by Jewish household ceremonial was no longer a factor.

[19] For a recent examination of the thesis that the biblical usage justifies our speaking of an *oikos*-formula see Peter Weigandt, "Zur sogenannten 'Oikosformel'" in *Novum Testamentum*, 6, 1 (Jan., 1963), 49-74. Weigandt joins K. Aland in his opposition to the *oikos*-formula thesis as developed especially by E. Stauffer and J. Jeremias. Gerhard Delling, however, gives more adequate consideration to the implications of the recurrence of the household terminology in early missions contexts; see his "Zur Taufe von 'Häusern' im Urchristentum" in *Novum Testamentum*, 7, 4 (Oct., 1965), 285-311.

authority principle of covenant administration the precise constituency of the households involved would not need to be determined. Whether or not there were infant children in one case or the other, or slaves in this or that household, households are mentioned along with the central authority figures in these instances, and these households had to consist of somebody in the category of household subordinates. Even with respect to the narrower question of whether parental authority is honored in the administration of the New Covenant, it would not matter whether conclusive evidence could be adduced proving that there were no children in any of these households; for if there were no children, then surely the households consisted of servants; and if it could be shown that servants were received into the church on the basis of the authority principle, it would follow *a fortiori* that the continuity with Old Testament practice included infants too. But what has to be determined is whether the household subordinates who were involved, of whatever variety, were received and baptized on the basis of personal conviction and confession or because they belonged to the household of one who confessed the Christian faith. And that is where certainty does not appear attainable.

The recurring mention of the household along with the central figure, whether in description of an existing God-fearing community, or in an invitation to salvation, or in an account of the acknowledgment of faith, or in a record of the administration of baptism, can very naturally be interpreted as the terminological reflex of a standard missions policy according to which the covenant community would regularly be enlarged through the accretion of household authority units. Indeed, it seems easier, particularly in the cases of prospective announcements of salvation and evangelistic proclamation (Acts 11:14; 16:31), to account for the recurrence of the appended reference to the household as a statement reflecting administrative policy rather than as a prediction based on a possible general rule that the sovereign soteric operations of the Spirit of God permeate intimate groupings of men. To explain the language of these declarations as meaning that the invitation with its terms was not confined to the householder but was extended to the members of his household, they, too, being invited to salvation on the same condition of faith,[20] seems some-

---

[20] So Beasley-Murray in *Baptism Today and Tomorrow* (New York, 1966), p. 121, following Alford, Haenchen, *et al.*

what artificial; moreover, it would not explain the phenomenon of recurrence.

Nevertheless, one is constrained to hold open the question whether in the administration of the New Covenant and particularly of the New Covenant's oath-sign of baptism the believing master's authority over his servant is to be reckoned as a covenantal authority. Clear New Testament statements such as we have in the case of the children of believers are not available to the effect that the covenantal authority of Christ reaches through Christian masters to claim the servants of their households. Even if the evidence be thought to suggest a continuity between Old and New Covenant practice in this regard, careful discrimination would be necessary in the identification of qualifying authority units amidst the multiform cultures encountered by the church in the penetration of the Christian mission to the ends of the earth. Special problems would also be posed for the exercise of church discipline, requiring definitions of individual responsibility answering to the terms of admission to baptism rather than to some age standard of accountability. That is, the liability of baptized adult household servants to church discipline, and also their commensurate privileges, especially that of access to the communion sacrament, would wait, as in the case of baptized children, for the individual confession of personal faith. Perhaps the complications that can easily be foreseen developing in this area are in themselves sufficient to turn us from further consideration of this approach as a proper interpretation of New Testament directives, or in any case to lead us to judge the procedure as generally inexpedient, should we be of the opinion that the New Testament at least permitted it. Certainly, no little wisdom would be required in order to apply this policy with foresighted regard to long-range missions strategy in different cultures undergoing continual modification throughout the church's age-long history. On the other hand, in certain societal formations the true progress of the gospel might conceivably be expedited if the church were free in its organizational process to employ the household authority principle. This governmental procedure would not need to be viewed as more than provisional, pending possible societal restructuring as the local culture was increasingly influenced by the total witness of the church in its midst. Meanwhile, a desirable measure of flexibility and adaptability would be afforded to the church in its missionary development.

It may be useful to see the operation of the authority principle in covenant administration in longer perspective. We shall therefore survey, if only in broadly analytical outline, the relation sustained by the covenant institution to other coexisting cultural authority structures in the successive epochs of covenant history. Special attention will be given to the nature of the sanctions employed in the several covenant administrations, an aspect of the matter that has particular relevance for the questions surrounding the application of the parental-householder authority principle to baptism.

In the beginning under the Covenant of Creation no distinction existed between the covenant institution and an extra-covenantal area of cultural authority structures. The universal community of man in all his cultural relationships constituted precisely the form of the authority structure of the covenant. It is an ultimate goal of the Covenant of Redemption to bring about once again a total and simple institutional identification of the covenant with the entire community of the new mankind in their consummated relationship to the whole new creation. That will be the final accomplishment of Christ, the Redeemer-King.

In the historical administrations of the Covenant of Redemption prior to that consummation there is never a simple identification of the covenant structure with the totality of the human cultural complex. This is not to deny that the servant of God fulfills his cultural vocation as a covenantal service in the name of his Lord, but it is to recognize that the Covenant of Redemption exists in this world at present as a distinct and limited organizational entity in the midst of other, non-covenantal institutions. Nor is the recognition of such non-covenantal institutions a denial of the lordship of Christ over all institutions; it simply distinguishes between the Covenant of Redemption as a specific historical program and confessional institution and the more fundamental and comprehensive Covenant of the Kingdom.[21] In terms of the latter Christ is Lord, yes, even covenantal Lord, over all.

But if there is not a total identification between the structure of the covenant and that of human culture, neither is there a complete separation between the two. The Covenant of Redemption in its organization and operation avails itself of the structures and processes in which man's cultural history unfolds. It does so, however, in different ways in different ages.

In Old Testament times the redemptive covenant actually em-

---

[21] *Cf.* above, Chapter Two, under "Covenant and Kingdom."

bodied itself in one or another cultural authority structure. These cultural units did not comprise the unbroken totality of culture as in the pre-redemptive age, but the covenant and the particular cultural unit did coalesce. As authority structures they were one and coextensive. Thus, the structure of the Abrahamic Covenant was identical with that of the patriarch's authority sphere. And since the covenant took over as its own structure the existing social structure with Abraham as head of the household-community, Abraham was also head over the covenantal community, and covenantal government included (even at the human level) cultural-physical sanctions.[22] In the course of time the patriarchal societal form was replaced by the kingdom of Israel, household authorities being now supplemented by various kingdom authorities. But the covenant structure was still one and the same as this more complex cultural form. In fact, it was the covenant revela-
form of Israel with a view to the typological purposes of the cove-
tion through Moses that had legislatively molded this cultural
nant and its history in that pre-messianic age.[23]

In New Testament times there is no longer a simple coalescence of the authority structure of the covenant with that of any cultural unit. Although the New Covenant honors parental (if not household) authority and works through it, the government of the New Covenant, even at the human level, is not limited to that (or to any more comprehensive) cultural form. For the New Covenant adds a system of special, strictly cultic officers as a second, and indeed dominant, focus of its human authority structure. The New Covenant thus has a cultural authority focus in the covenant family and a cultic authority focus in the assembled, worshipping congregation with its special officers.

The latter feature is a significantly new development in the pattern of covenant authority. The Mosaic Covenant, too, had its special authorities in addition to the parent-householders of Israel, but that additional authority was not of a non-cultural nature. For it was the authority of a visible, earthly kingdom and as such it had recourse to economic and corporal, including capital, sanctions. The kingdom of Israel was, of course, not another Caesar-kingdom but, uniquely, the kingdom of God institutionally

---

[22] Illustrative episodes from the patriarchal era would be those recorded in Gen. 16:6ff.; 21:14; 27:28f., 39f.; 38:24; 49:2ff.

[23] See the Deuteronomic stipulations regulative of Israel's government, especially 17:14ff. *Cf.* I Sam. 10:17ff.

present among the nations. Its earthly cultural form was symbolic of the ultimate integration of culture and cult in the world of the consummation. The judicial infliction of cultural sanctions by its officers typified the final messianic judgment of men in the totality of their being as cultural creatures. This institutional symbolization of the final judgment and eternal kingdom disappeared from the earthly scene when the Old Covenant gave way to the New. In this age of the church, royal theocratic authority with its prerogative of imposing physical-cultural sanctions resides solely in Christ, the heavenly King. The judicial authority of the permanent special officers whom Christ has appointed to serve his church on earth is purely spiritual-cultic.

Cultural sanctions have no place, therefore, in the functioning of the central and dominant cultic authority focus of the New Covenant community, and it would violate the spirit of the church's distinctive mission in the present age if such sanctions were to be introduced in connection with the auxiliary family (-household) focus of authority. The discordance would be especially jarring and in fact quite intolerable in the case of the master's enforcement of his authority over his slave, since violations of this fundamentally civic-economic form of authority would be judicable in civil court and punishable by the sword of the state. Do we, then, encounter here a difficulty that would render impracticable the integration of covenant authority with family (-household) authority in this present age?

As previously observed, covenant viewed as the total lordship of Christ over the lives of his individual servants spans the kingdom-cultural and the church-cultic spheres. Moreover, the institution of the covenant family spans these two spheres. Nevertheless, until the eschatological reintegration of culture and cultus on a universal scale, the individual servant of Christ must distinguish between those functions he performs as a member of the church (*i.e.*, of the covenant as institution in the total unity of its dual foci of authority) and his more general kingdom activities. He must do so even within the life of his covenant family, distinguishing between those aspects of it that are covenantal in the institutional sense and those that are covenantal only in the broader kingdom sense. One aspect of it requiring such analysis is the disciplinary exercise of parental(-household) authority. Now surely the parent's chastening of covenant children is not to be equated with church discipline. Similarly, then, if the policy of household incorporation into the covenant were being practiced, a Philemon's civil dealings with an offending Onesimus (the question of a better way for the moment aside) would have to be and could readily be distinguished from ecclesiastical discipline. Thus, under the New Covenant, the cultural authority structure of the family(-household) is to be utilized in the incorporation of members into the covenant but not for the administration of the judicial discipline of the covenant. The latter is the province of the church's special officers, whose authority and discipline are exclusively cultic-spiritual.

Conclusions: The administration of baptism as the sign of demarcation of the congregation of the New Covenant takes account both of personal confession and of the confessor's temporal authority. Just as there had to be an Abraham as the confessing nucleus of the Abrahamic covenant community marked by circumcision, so there had to be a nuclear company of disciples who confessed Christ as Lord for the establishment of the church of the New Covenant sealed by baptism. So, too, in the continuing mission of that church among new families and peoples, the administering of the sign of covenantal incorporation awaits the emergence of the confession of Christ's lordship. But though the confession of faith has this primacy in the administration of baptism it is not the exclusive principle regulative of this rite. For the one who confesses Christ is required to fulfill his responsibility with respect to those whom God has placed under his parental (if not household) authority, exercising that authority to consecrate his charges with himself to the service of Christ. The basis for the baptism of the children of believers is thus simply their parents' covenantal authority over them.

For those who are baptized according to the secondary principle of authority as well as for those who are baptized according to the primary principle of confession, baptism is a sign of incorporation within the judicial sphere of Christ's covenant lordship for a final verdict of blessing or curse. In the one case the reception of baptism is a matter of active commitment; in the other, of passive consecration. But in every instance, to be baptized is to be consigned by oath to the Lord of redemptive judgment.

INDEXES

I. INDEX OF SCRIPTURE REFERENCES

Genesis
1	26f., 30
1:28	17 n. 8
2	26f., 27 n. 3, 30
3	26, 27 n. 3
3:15	30
3:24	69
6:2	66 n. 6
6:4f.	66 n. 6
6:13	66 n. 6
8:21–9:17	27
8:22	27
9	31 n. 4
9:11	62 n. 24
13:15	22
15	16f., 19, 24, 34, 42, 45, 61, 71
15:5	17
15:7	40
15:9ff.	42 n. 9
15:9-11	17
15:13	22
15:14	17
15:16	17
15:17	17
15:18	42 n. 9
15:18ff.	17, 17 n. 8
16:6ff.	100 n. 22
17	24 n. 17, 39ff., 39 n. 1, 45
17:1	40
17:2	40
17:4-8	40
17:7	40, 88
17:9-14	40, 43
17:12	88
17:12f.	88
17:14	40, 43, 62 n. 24
17:15-21	40
17:23	88
17:23-27	40
17:27	88
21:4	44
21:14	100 n. 22
22	45
22:1ff.	44
27:28f.	100 n. 22
27:39f.	100 n. 22
35:2ff.	94
38:24	100 n. 22
46:2ff.	22
49:2ff.	100 n. 22

Exodus
4:21-23	89
4:23	89 n. 11
4:24-26	88, 89 n. 10
12:7	89 n. 11
12:22	89 n. 11
12:40ff.	22
13:21f.	68
14:19f.	68
14:20	68, 68 n. 13
14:24ff.	68
15:13ff.	56 n. 9
19–24	18
19:5, 6	18
19:6	92
19:18	68
20:12	94
24	17
24:5ff.	18
24:7	17
24:16f.	68
33:19	68
34:28	20

Leviticus
18:5	22
19:23-25	44, 54
26:41	47

Numbers
5	55, 72
12:10	68
14:10ff.	68

103

15:20	92	*Ezra*	
16:19	68	9:1ff.	95
16:42	68		
20:6	68	*Nehemiah*	
		10:28f.	94
Deuteronomy		10:30	95
4:13	20	13:23ff.	95
10:4	20		
10:16	47	*Psalms*	
17:14ff.	100	2:7f.	59
26:17ff.	19	18:6	59 n. 19
26:17-19	19	18:15f.	59 n. 17
27:15-26	19	18:20-24	59 n. 19
28:3-6	88	37:9ff.	56 n. 9
28:9f.	80	37:22	56 n. 9
28:16-19	88	37:33f.	56 n. 9
28:26	17 n. 7	42	59 n. 19
29:10a	19	42:7	59 n. 17
29:10ff.	94	43	60 n. 19
29:10-15	85 n. 2	43:1	59 n. 19
29:12a	19	50:5	18
29:12	42	68:22	59 n. 17
29:14	19	69	59, 60 n. 19
30:1-10	75	69:1f.	59
30:6	47	69:14f.	59
32:40	19, 33 n. 5	74:12-15	60
32:40ff.	19	89:3	20
		89:9f.	60
Joshua		105:9, 10	22
2:10f.	56 n. 9	124:4f.	59 n. 17
5	42 n. 11	132:11	20
5:1	56 n. 9	144:7	59 n. 17
5:2ff.	43 n. 11		
5:13	42 n. 11	*Isaiah*	
7:14	55 n. 7	4:2-5	68
12ff.	17 n. 8	5:1ff.	53
24	17 n. 8, 20	11:10-16	56 n. 10
24:2ff.	40 n. 2	27:1	56 n. 10
24:15b-24	20	27:12f.	56 n. 10
24:24	20	40:3	53 n. 4
24:25	20, 20 n. 12	42:1	58 n. 14
		43:1	28
I Samuel		43:1-3a	61
10:17ff.	100	43:15	28
17:44ff.	17 n. 7	51:9f.	60
17:54	72	51:10f.	56 n. 10
		53:8b	46
II Samuel		63:19	80 n. 32
7:15ff.	20		
		Jeremiah	
I Kings		4:4	43, 47
8:31f.	59 n. 19	6:10	47

9:25, 26	47	8:12	77
31	75	11:14	54
31:31ff.	74ff., 75 n. 23, 76 n. 26	12:39f.	60
		13:24-30	78
34:18	42 n. 9	13:36-43	78
34:19f.	17 n. 7	13:47-49	78
		13:49	69
Ezekiel		17:12f.	54
28:10	43 n. 11	19:13-15	93
31:18	43 n. 11	21:23	53
32:10ff.	43 n. 11	21:23-32	52
36:25	54 n. 6	21:23ff.	64
		21:31	69
Daniel		21:33ff.	52
7:9f.	58 n. 13	21:40, 41	53
7:11	58 n. 13	21:42f.	53
7:26f.	58 n. 13	22:2ff.	52 n. 3
9:26f.	62	24:51	43 n. 11
		25:1-30	78
Jonah		26:31f.	49 n. 21
1:7	55 n. 7	28:18-20	79
2:1ff.	60		
		Mark	
Zechariah		1:3	53 n. 4
10:10f.	56 n. 10	1:4	54
11	64 n. 2	1:8	57
13:1	54 n. 6	1:10f.	59
13:7	49	1:14f.	64
13:8	49	1:15	64
13:9	49	9:7	69 n. 16
		9:12f.	54
Malachi		10:13-16	93
3:1	53	10:38	59
3:2ff.	54, 58	11:22ff.	64
4:1, 2	58	11:27-33	52
4:4-6	54 n. 5	11:28	53
4:5, 6	54	12:1ff.	52
		12:10f.	53
Matthew		13:27	69
3:2	54	14:27f.	49 n. 21
3:3	53 n. 4		
3:7ff.	54	*Luke*	
3:10	62	1:17	54
3:11	58, 59 n. 15, 69 n. 16	1:35	69 n. 16
		1:72f.	24 n. 18
3:11, 12	51, 57	3:3	54
3:12	59 n. 15	3:4	53 n. 4
3:16f.	59	3:5ff.	66 n. 7
4:8ff.	59	3:7ff.	54
4:12ff.	64	3:9	62
4:17	64	3:16	59 n. 15
7:21-23	78	3:16f.	57

3:17	59 n. 15
3:18	57
3:22	59
4:5ff.	59
4:14	64
4:19	64
4:21	64
10:24	76
12:49	59 n. 15
12:50	59, 70
12:51ff.	59 n. 15
18:15-17	93
20:1ff.	64
20:1-8	52
20:2	53
20:9ff.	52
20:17f.	53

John

1:23	53 n. 4
1:29-34	58 n. 14
1:32f.	59
3:17	34
3:18	34
3:22	63
4:1	64 n. 2, 80 n. 30
4:1f.	63
4:1-3	64
4:53	96
15:1-8	77

Acts

1:5	78
1:18	43 n. 11
2:17	85 n. 2
2:38	80
2:38ff.	96
2:39	85 n. 2
2:40f.	66, 66 n. 7
3:25	24 n. 18
7:51	47
8:16	80
10:2	96
10:37	64
10:47f.	96
11:14	96f.
16:15	96
16:31	97
16:33ff.	96
18:8	96
19:5	80
22:16	83 n. 42

Romans

1:4	59 n. 16
2:25-29	47
3:26	30
3:31	30
4:11	47
4:25b	73
5	28
5:13, 14	28
5:14	28
5:18-21	31
5:19	29
5:20	28f.
6	30
6:3ff.	70f., 73
6:3, 4	46
6:6	46 n. 16, 71
10:9	80
11	62, 92 n. 15
11:16	92
11:17-21	77
11:17ff.	92 n. 15
13:4	42 n. 11
14:10	78

I Corinthians

1:13	70
1:13ff.	80
1:16	96
7	95
7:12ff.	95
7:14	91ff., 92 n. 15
7:39	95
10:1ff.	58 n. 13, 67
10:2	57, 68ff., 69 n. 15
11:27	80 n. 35
12:13	69 n. 16
15	28f.
15:42-50	29

II Corinthians

3:3	75
3:6ff.	25
5:10	78

Galatians

2:20	46 n. 16
3	24, 28f.
3:12	22
3:15ff.	22, 25
3:17	22
3:18	29, 31

3:18a	22	*Hebrews*	
3:29	29	6:4ff.	77
4:24	25	6:17, 18	16
5:24	46 n. 16	9:18ff.	18
6:12-15	46 n. 16	10:26-31	80 n. 35
		11:7	66 n. 4
Ephesians		11:19	46 n. 14
1:13f.	80	12:18-29	68
2:15f.	71		
4:5	80	*I Peter*	
4:30	80	1:10-12	76
5:26	83 n. 42	3:20	65 n. 3, 66
6:1-3	94	3:20-22	65
6:4	94	3:21	57, 65ff., 65 n. 3, 67 n. 8, 80, 80 n. 35
6:12	73	3:22	66f.
Philippians			
3:3	47	*II Peter*	
		2:5	66
Colossians		2:7	66
1:22	45, 71	3:5-7	55
2	46, 72		
2:11	45, 46 n. 15, 71, 73	*I John*	
2:11f.	46, 67 n. 9, 73	3:8	34
2:11ff.	47, 59 n. 16, 70		
2:12	71	*Revelation*	
2:13ff.	47 n. 17	1:13ff.	68 n. 12
2:14	72	1:15f.	68 n. 12
2:15	46 n. 15, 72f., 73 n. 21	2	77
		3	77
3:5-9	46f.	7:2ff.	80
3:9	46 n. 15, 71	12	60 n. 20
3:11	45	12:7ff.	72
3:20	94	14:1	80
		15	68
I Timothy		15:1	69
6:12	81 n. 38	15:2	69, 69 n. 15
		15:8	69
II Timothy		16	69
1:16	96	17:1	69
2:19	80	19:15f.	42 n. 11
4:19	96	20:9ff.	58 n. 13
		21:9	69
Titus		22:4	80
3:5	83 n. 42		

II. INDEX OF NAMES AND SUBJECTS

Abban, 87
Abraham, 16, 18, 22, 24, 29, 39f., 44ff., 54, 57, 61f., 87ff., 100
Abrahamic Covenant, 16ff., 22, 39ff., 48, 88, 100
Adam, 26ff., 32, 35, 44, 46, 48
Allegory, 25, 60
Ark of the Covenant, 24
Ashurnirari V, 41, 87

Baal Epic, 52 n. 2
Babylon, 69
Baptism: administration of, 90ff.; Christian, 63ff.; incorporation into covenant, 79ff., 91, 94, 102; Johannine, 50ff.; mode of, 69f., 82f.; sign of judgment, 51, 54, 58f., 61f., 63, 66ff., 70ff., 78f., 81; symbolic water ordeal, 55ff., 59f., 61, 65f., 67f., 78, 82f.; Reformed view of, 50, 83
Bar-Ga'ayah, 17
Belt-Wrestling, 73

Canaan(ites), 43 n. 11, 56
Children, 88, 90ff.
Church Liturgies, 60, 70 n. 18, 81 n. 38
Circumcision, 39ff., 54, 57, 61 n. 22, 62, 62 n. 24, 71, 73, 81f., 84, 86ff., 90 n. 12
Common Grace, 31 n. 4, 99f.
Consecration, 36ff., 41, 43ff., 47, 65, 67, 81f., 84, 88f., 102
Covenant, Definition of, 16, 29ff., 33ff., 36ff., 74, 79
Covenant of Creation, 30, 33, 36f., 74, 79
Covenant of Grace, 27, 35f.
Covenant of Redemption, 29, 31ff., 37, 47, 74, 80, 84, 99
Covenant of the Kingdom, 37, 99
Covenant of Works, 32, 36
Covenant Theology, 14ff., 26, 31, 34f.

Damascus Document, 77, 77 n. 28, 96 n. 18

David, 19, 72
Davidic Covenant, 19f.
Death-Burial-Resurrection, 46f., 70ff., 82 n. 40
Decalogue, 20, 23, 38 n. 10, 39f.
Deluge, 55ff., 62 n. 24, 65ff., 67 n. 9, 83
Deuteronomic Covenant, 17 n. 8, 18ff., 32
Duppi-Tessub, 86

Eden, 28, 33
Egypt(ians), 22, 56, 68
El, 52 n. 2
Election, 13, 28, 31ff., 44, 74, 79
Esarhaddon, 17, 53 n. 4, 85, 87
Ezra, 95

Fire, 49, 57f., 58 n. 13, 59 n. 15, 61, 68f., 71, 77f., 83 n. 41

Galilee, 64, 64 n. 2
Gehenna, 57
Golgotha, 45
Goliath, 72

Hagar, 25
Hammurapi (and Code of), 37f., 38 n. 9, 44 n. 13, 55
Horeb, 54 n. 5
Household, 24, 39, 65, 88f., 91ff., 96 n. 19, 100ff.

Iarimlim, 87
Isaac, 22, 44ff.
Ishmael, 88
Israel, 14f., 17ff., 28, 32, 52ff., 56f., 61f., 63f., 64 n. 2, 69f., 70 n. 17, 76ff., 89, 92, 95, 100, 100 n. 23

Jacob, 22
Jericho, 38
Jerusalem (Zion), 53, 68f.
Jesus Christ: and law, 23, 30f., 33, 74; baptism of, 58f., 61; circumcision of, 45; covenant messenger, 52f., 63f.; covenant servant, 58, 58 n. 14, 74; death ordeal of,

INDEXES 109

45f., 49, 58, 60, 70ff., 79; King-Judge, 37 n. 9, 57f., 62, 68 n. 12, 77f., 99, 101; Lamb of God, 58; Lord of Church, 51, 63, 65, 80f., 82, 93f., 98, 102; mission of, 34; Redeemer-Substitute, 48, 79; resurrection of, 46f., 49, 67, 70ff.; second Adam (and federal representative), 28f., 31f., 35, 74; temptation of, 59
John the Baptist, 50ff., 56ff., 63f., 66 n. 7, 78
Jonah, 59f., 83
Jordan, 56f., 60f., 83
Josephus, 81
Joshua, 20, 56

Kashtiliash, 48 n. 19

Law, 13ff., 22ff., 27ff., 33, 36, 48, 74f.
Lawsuit, Covenant, 51ff., 52 n. 2, 58, 61f., 63f., 77 n. 29
Leviathan (Dragon), 52 n. 2, 60
Lord's Supper, 67, 81 n. 35, 98
Lutheran Theology, 13, 13 n. 1

Malachi, 54 n. 5
Marriage and Covenant, 91ff., 94f.
Mati'el (Mati'ilu), 17, 41f., 87
Moab, 19
Moriah, 45f.
Moses, 22f., 32f., 37f., 52, 56, 67ff., 75 n. 25, 88f., 100
Mursilis, 86

Nazareth, 64
Nazirites, 38
Nehemiah, 95
New Covenant, 33, 36, 64f., 73ff., 75 n. 23, 76 n. 26, 77 n. 27, 91, 94, 97f., 100ff.
Ninurta, 17
Niqmad, 52 n. 2
Noah, 27, 66
Noahic Covenant, 27

Oath, 16ff., 24, 30, 32f., 38, 41ff., 61, 67, 71, 77, 80f., 81 nn. 37, 38, 39, 85ff., 94f., 102
Onesimus, 102

Ordeal, Judicial, 48, 52, 54ff., 61f., 65ff., 72f., 81ff.

Passover, 42 n. 8, 89 n. 11
Pentecost, 66, 78, 83 n. 41
Persian Eschatology, 57
Pharisees, 64 n. 2
Philemon, 102
Pliny, 81 n. 38
Promise, 13ff., 22ff., 29ff., 33, 40, 87
Prophets, 51f.

Qumran, 53 n. 4, 54, 57, 59, 77, 81

Ramataia, 85, 87
Ratification Rites, 16ff., 16 n. 6, 24, 30, 38, 39ff., 47, 89, 92 n. 14
Red Sea, 56, 60f., 67 n. 10, 68ff., 69 n. 15, 70 nn. 17 and 18, 83
Reformed Theology, 13f., 36, 50

Sacramentum, 81
Sarah, 25, 40, 87
Satan, 34, 49 n. 20, 57, 59f., 72
Seal, 50, 57, 79f., 90, 102
Shechem, 20
Shuppiluliuma, 52 n. 2
Sinaitic Covenant, 14, 16 n. 6, 17ff., 21ff., 30, 32, 35 n. 6, 36 n. 7, 38 n. 10, 52, 54 n. 5, 61, 68, 75, 92 n. 14, 94, 100
Slaves, 88, 94ff., 101f.
Spirit, Holy, 57f., 59, 69 n. 16, 78f., 83 n. 41, 97

Theocracy, 90 n. 12, 92, 100f.
Theophany, 16, 42 n. 11, 45, 61, 68ff., 68 n. 12, 71f., 77
Treaties, 14, 17, 20f., 27, 31, 37, 38 n. 10, 39ff., 40 n. 3, 48 n. 19, 51, 55, 77 n. 28, 80, 84ff., 88, 91
Tudhaliyas IV, 87
Tukulti-Ninurta, 48 n. 19

Ugarit, 52 n. 2, 55 n. 8
Ulmi-Teshub, 87
Urim and Thummim, 55 n. 7
Ur-Nammu, 55

Yamm, 52 n. 2, 55 n. 8

Zipporah, 89 n. 11

III. INDEX OF AUTHORS

Aland, K., 96 n. 19
Alonso-Schökel, L., 27 n. 3
Anderson, B. W., 76 n. 26

Baltzer, K., 17 n. 8, 77 n. 28
Bandstra, A. J., 72 n. 20
Beasley-Murray, G. R., 63 n. 1, 92 n. 15, 97 n. 20
Begrich, J., 15 n. 4
Betz, O., 43 n. 11
Blanchette, O. A., 72 n. 20
Brownlee, W. H., 53 n. 4, 57 n. 12
Bruce, F. F., 71 n. 19
Bultmann, R., 75 n. 23

Calvin, J., 22
Cazelles, M., 19 n. 11
Childs, B. S., 76 n. 26
Copisarow, M., 70 n. 17
Coppens, J., 75 n. 24
Cullmann, O., 58 n. 14

Davies, W. D., 75 n. 25
Delling, G., 96 n. 19
Dillistone, F. W., 83 n. 43

Eichrodt, W., 14f., 20 n. 13, 27 n. 2, 36 n. 7, 37 n. 8
Eissfeldt, O., 43 n. 11

Farrer, A., 69 n. 15
Fensham, F. C., 42 n. 8

Glasson, T. F., 75 n. 25
Goetze, A., 86 n. 5
Gordon, C. H., 55 n. 8, 73 n. 21

Harvey, J., 52 n. 2
Hillers, D. R., 17 n. 7, 41 n. 5, 42 n. 9

Jeremias, J., 96 n. 19
Jewett, P. K., 77 n. 27, 90 n. 12

Käsemann, E., 69 n. 15
Kitchen, K. A., 21 n. 14, 40 n. 3
Kline, M. G., 17 nn. 8 and 9, 33 n. 5, 39 n. 1, 52 n. 2, 66 n. 6, 70 n. 18, 73 n. 21

Kosmala, H., 88 n. 10
Kraetzschmar, R., 14, 15 n. 2
Külling, S. R., 39 n. 1

Lampe, G. W. H., 80 n. 34
Lundberg, P., 60 n. 21, 67 n. 9, 69 nn. 15 and 16, 70 n. 18

Marcel, P. C., 77 n. 27
McCarthy, D. J., 16 n. 6, 19 n. 11, 21 n. 14, 38 n. 10, 40 n. 3, 41 n. 6, 42 nn. 7 and 9, 48 n. 19, 85 n. 1, 86 n. 4, 87 nn. 7 and 9
Mendenhall, G. E., 42 n. 8, 80 n. 35
Moule, C. F. D., 50 n. 1
Munn-Rankin, J. M., 85 n. 1
Murray, J., 15 n. 5, 18 n. 10, 82 n. 40

Neufeld, V. H., 80 n. 31

Rad, G. von, 20 n. 13, 21, 25 n. 19
Reicke, B., 66 n. 5, 67 n. 8
Ridderbos, H., 35 n. 6
Roehrs, W. R., 13 n. 1
Rowley, H. H., 67 n. 10

Schmidt, H., 60 n. 19
Schnackenburg, R., 70 n. 18, 82 n. 40
Selwyn, E. G., 67 n. 8
Speiser, E. A., 68 n. 13
Stauffer, E., 96 n. 19
Strack, H. L., Billerbeck, P., 95 n. 17, 96 n. 18

Towers, J. R., 70 n. 17

Victor, P., 20 n. 12
Vos, G., 16 n. 6
Vos, L. A., 69 n. 14

Weigandt, P., 96 n. 19
White, R. E. O., 77 n. 27
Wingren, G., 13 n. 1
Wiseman, D. J., 53 n. 4, 85 n. 2, 86 n. 3, 87 nn. 6 and 8